BELVA LOCKWOOD

EQUAL RIGHTS PIONEER

Jill Norgren

Twenty-First Century Books / Minneapolis

For Elena, Ilomai, and Isabel, with love

Acknowledgments: Barbara Allen Babcock, Wendy Chmielewski, Robert Ellis, Ann Gordon, and Norma Wollenberg, for their expertise; Betsy Gitter, Serena Nanda, and Philippa Strum for their encouraging words; Cecelia Cancellaro for getting me to the starting gate; Sheila Cole and Meg Fidler for help on early drafts; Marcia Marshall and Martha Kranes for helping me to tell the story well; Ralph, Tiana, Chris, Anneka, and Luis, for their love and humor; and pioneering women everywhere, for their insight and courage.

Twenty-First Century Books
A division of Lerner Publishing Group, Inc.
241 First Avenue North
Minneapolis, MN 55401 U.S.A.

Website address: www.lernerbooks.com

Library of Congress Cataloging-in-Publication Data

Norgren, Jill.
    Belva Lockwood : equal rights pioneer / by Jill Norgren.
        p.   cm. — (Trailblazer biographies)
    Includes bibliographical references and index.
    ISBN 978–0–8225–9068–2 (lib. bdg. : alk. paper)
    1. Lockwood, Belva Ann, 1830–1917. 2. Lawyers—United States—Biography. 3. Women lawyers—United States—Biography. 4. Women's rights—United States—Biography. 5. Women—United States—Biography. I. Title.
    KF368.L58N667 2009
    340.092—dc22 [B]   2007050265

Manufactured in the United States of America
1 2 3 4 5 6 – BP – 14 13 12 11 10 09

CONTENTS

AUTHOR'S NOTE

Some biographical figures are easier to write about than others. Attorney Belva Lockwood (1830–1917) proved to be one of the difficult ones. Although she was a well-known advocate for the equal rights of women, following her death, most of her letters, personal journals, and law office logbooks were destroyed. She had outlived her husband and daughters. Her remaining family did not understand her importance and did not save her papers.

In order to write her story, I had to become a detective. I was convinced that Lockwood, as the first woman to practice before the U.S. Supreme Court and the first woman to run a full campaign for the presidency, must have left some footprints. I turned to library guides to discover where there might be information about her. Lockwood moved to Washington, D.C., in 1866. I went to Washington and snooped around the local libraries and historical societies as well as the Library of Congress and the National Archives. A librarian at the National Archives gave me great advice: "Lockwood was a lawyer. Ask to see the docket books [record books] of the Washington, D.C., courts in the years that she practiced law because her name will be listed next to the entry for any legal case in which she was the attorney of record." I spent three months turning the pages of dusty docket books, looking for her name and the details of the cases that she handled. When the dust got too much for my allergies, I walked up Capitol Hill to the beautiful Library of Congress where I read newspaper articles published during Lockwood's lifetime that described her involvement in the women's rights movement, her political campaigns, and her peace activism. At this library, I also discovered important letters that Lockwood had written to several presidents.

I was also very careful to tell anyone who would listen that I wanted to write about Lockwood. This led to more clues, as helpful teachers, authors, and librarians suggested where I might find more letters and personal papers. One day at the National Archives, another librarian said that he had a distant cousin, now dead, who had done business with Lockwood. He told me to look for letters written by her at Duke University's manuscripts library in North Carolina. Those letters turned out to be important in understanding Lockwood's legal work for the Cherokee people. Another tip gave me the name and telephone number of an elderly woman in California whose husband was a distant relation of Lockwood's second husband. On the phone, this kind woman told me that they proudly displayed framed letters and business certificates of Lockwood's that had never been seen by anyone outside of the family. When she realized that I lived three thousand miles away, she got into her car, drove to a mall, and made copies of everything about Lockwood in her home.

Like all biographers, I had hoped to find photographs of Lockwood and her family. I wanted to get to know Lockwood, her children, and her husband through pictures. I wanted to see Lockwood on the campaign trail and in court. I looked for photos in all the libraries that I visited. As it turned out, I was not lucky. Photography was only invented in the 1820s, and the newspapers that covered her achievements did not regularly print photographs until the end of that century. The average American household did not own a camera because cameras were expensive. In Lockwood's day, a family had to travel to a photographer's studio and pay a fair amount of money for a keepsake picture. Still, Belva Lockwood came from a large family and I keep hoping that in some old attic or basement, we will eventually find more photographs of her and the people she loved and, of course, more letters and maybe some diaries.

—Jill Norgren

CHAPTER ONE

REBEL

Mud squished between ten-year-old Belva's toes. Earlier, without telling anyone her plans, she had quietly closed the door of her parents' small farmhouse and walked to the nearby pond. She did not ask any of her sisters or even her little brother, Warren, to come with her. This was secret business.

Belva Bennett was a very confident girl. She was smart and athletic and did not frighten easily. She had made up her mind to try something that seemed scary, even to her. She was going to test the strength of her religious faith. Like Peter in the Bible, she would try to walk on water.

Standing at the edge of the pond, Belva looked down and saw the little minnow fish that she often tried to catch in her hands. Like any proper nineteenth-century girl, she was wearing a skirt that fell to her ankles. This was so even though she lived on a farm and regularly cleaned up after cows and hauled firewood full of sawdust. How much easier life would be if she could wear trousers like Warren did. Still, water or no water, she did not dare to remove her clothes. Of course, if she were successful, they would not get wet.

Belva did not wait long before nervously raising one foot above the water. She had read the Bible carefully, and she believed in miracles. "If the sea could hold up Peter," she thought, "surely a pond would hold up a little girl." She held her breath and quickly moved her foot downward. For one moment, she imagined that her faith had lifted her up. Then she felt the cold pond water soak through her skirt.

Dejected, splattered with mud, and wet to her waist, Belva walked home and faced a scolding from her mother. But one reprimand about muddy clothes did not stop Belva from stubbornly trying to repeat other biblical miracles, such as moving mountains (really, a small hill) and raising the dead. She tested herself in these ways. But she said nothing, afraid of what people would think.

Young Belva would have performed her chores wearing long skirts and dresses, just as this nineteenth-century American illustration shows.

After many failures, Belva gave up her efforts at miracle making. A few years later, as a teenager, she would realize that these adventures had been a bit silly. Still, she did not stop believing that difficult things were possible.

Belva Bennett was born on October 24, 1830, in western New York State. At that time, most people, including Belva's family, lived on farms and raised their own food. There were no corner stores, much less supermarkets, and the general store was far away. Women and girls spent long evening hours in the poor light of oil lamps, sewing and knitting the family's clothes. This was after the baking, butter churning, laundry, weeding, and baby care were finished. Farm animals lived close by, and children learned about birth and death from watching over them. To go to the bathroom, everyone trudged to an outhouse. Indoor toilets were unheard of in the country.

People in cities and towns lived differently from farm families, like Belva's. In the 1830s, cities were crowded, bustling places full of shops, factories, and warehouses—and an occasional wandering pig ate the garbage residents threw into the street. Fireplace chimneys belched smoke and soot into the air, and the wooden wheels of carts and carriages made an endless racket. City men, women, and children worked for pay and bought, rather than raised, the food they ate. Slavery wasn't common in the western settlements, but in the East and particularly the South, much of the work was done by slaves.

Farm and factory life demanded hard work from

women, but the customs and laws of the times denied them many opportunities. They could not get as much education as boys and men. They could not compete for the same jobs. When men and women married, the law required a wife to give her earnings to her husband—if the husband permitted her to work at all. By law, men were the heads of families and women were dependent on them, just like children.

Andrew Jackson was elected president of the United States shortly before Belva was born. He was a tall, handsome man with strong views about how to govern the nation. At the time, only white men who owned property were able to vote. Jackson thought that this was unfair. He felt that men should be able to vote whether they owned property or not. But it didn't bother him that women, rich or poor, were not allowed to vote at all. And so when Belva was a girl, her father, Lewis Bennett, could vote. Her mother, Hannah, who worked on the family farm next to her husband while raising five children, could not. She was not permitted to have her say in who was elected and how her tax money was spent. The law assumed that Lewis would speak for his wife.

Lewis and Hannah Bennett were among the first Americans to settle in Niagara County on land that earlier had been taken from the area's Native Americans. The snowy, cold upstate New York winters were hard to endure. But in springtime, the air turned soft and sweet. The green fields and forests promised plentiful crops, pastureland, and wood for heating and for building houses.

An illustration from 1849 shows Niagara Falls in upstate New York around the time Belva and her family lived in the area.

The Bennetts married when Lewis was twenty and Hannah was fifteen. They cleared land and planted crops. Despite how hard they worked, they never had much money.

When Hannah was sixteen, she gave birth to her first child, Rachel. Belva arrived two years later, followed by Warren, Cyrene, and Inverno, the baby of the family.

Belva was the bold, confident one. She was the star pupil at the little schoolhouse the Bennett children attended. Like other boys and girls in country schools across America, Belva's school was a one-room building crammed with children of all ages. A single teacher tried to keep order, often with the use of a wooden paddle. It was not an easy place to spend the day. There was constant noise, and according to the season, the room was either too hot or too cold. Still, Belva had no trouble with her grammar, math, and geography lessons. Book learning came easily to her.

Belva also loved the outdoors. She claimed to row a boat as well as any of the local boys, and she was an excellent horseback rider. She was always strong and healthy. With only one young brother in the family, Belva's parents gave her the job of caring for the farm animals. She complained later that her parents did not appreciate how well she performed boys' work.

Most of the children in Belva's small village only went to the district school for a few years. And they only went during the months when they were not needed for farm chores. By their middle teens, the boys had to begin full-time work on a farm or at the sawmill. The mill was a dangerous and noisy place, where tall trees from nearby forests were cut into lumber.

Girls, even the smartest students like Belva, also stopped school at a young age. They were expected to help their mothers and to prepare for marriage. Belva was fourteen when her parents decided that she should leave school and help the family by getting a job. Fortunately, members of the local school board saw Belva's abilities and asked her to become a teacher.

Belva's childhood ended when she took her place at the front of the classroom, facing the benches filled with her friends and younger siblings. She was happy to have a job that kept her near books, but the change from student to teacher was not an easy one. Discipline was a constant problem in every country school. Belva faced a room full of giggling six- and seven-year-olds and gossiping teenagers. Even though she was physically strong, it is unlikely that the paddle was her first choice for dealing with mischief makers. Women teachers like Belva were more likely to discipline their students with words or by ordering them to wear a dunce cap. Nobody liked sitting still at the front of the class wearing the tall, pointed hat with the word *dunce* on it.

Belva was not trained to be a teacher, but she was good at the subjects she taught. She knew what to

American oil painter Henry Inman portrayed an October school day at a one-room schoolhouse in 1845. Belva attended and later taught in one-room schoolhouses such as this.

expect from the students, having grown up with most of them. She continued to live at home, but her parents let her be more independent. This made her feel grown up. She was pleased with her new life. She even began to dream about enrolling in a ladies' seminary, a school for older girls who were good at their studies.

Her happiness ended one day when Belva discovered that the school board was paying her only half the salary of young male teachers. At home, her own father had made it clear to her time and time again that he did not think women should have the same opportunities as men. Still, Belva had never suffered this sort of treatment from people outside of her family. In her eyes, being paid so much less for the same work, only because she was a woman, was "an indignity."

She looked for a way to shame the people of her town, just as she shamed the students who misbehaved in her schoolroom. Off she marched to the house of a local minister. His wife invited her in. Once inside, Belva, who was anything but shy, complained loudly about being paid less than male teachers. Her hostess, probably surprised to hear a fifteen-year-old girl finding fault with her elders, listened carefully. She looked Belva in the eye and told her that such a practice was simply "the way of the world."

To Belva, this thinking was absurd and wrong. She left the minister's house determined to speak out, despite her youth and the possibility she would be fired. And speak out she did. Her protest did not change her pay, but it was the beginning of the behavior that Belva

Belva was outraged that she received half the salary of male teachers in the area.

would follow all her life. Whenever she learned about injustice, she refused to remain silent. She spoke out in public, even if it made her enemies.

The issue of her paycheck taught Belva that the world was not a perfect place. In 1776 the men who wrote the Declaration of Independence stated that all men are created equal. But in the 1840s, when Belva was a teenager, slavery was still practiced in the United States. Land was being taken from Native Americans so families like Belva's could start farms. Women could not control many aspects of their lives. They regularly lost their wages to their husbands and often, in divorces, the custody of their children. And, of course, women could not vote.

Many of the things Belva learned about a woman's role disturbed her. At night, in her bed, she began to imagine a different life. She loved her mother and aunts, but she did not want to live as they did. She began to dream of being someone different from the farm women she knew. She read the stories of the United States' early political leaders—George Washington, John Adams, Thomas Jefferson, and Daniel Webster. The lives of these great politicians and lawyers—men who helped to lead the United States and make it a better place—appealed to her. She began to picture herself as a woman who would do great things. This was a big dream for a young woman at that time.

Very few young people finished high school or went to college in those days, but Belva believed that she needed more schooling if she was to realize her dreams. She was ready to give up teaching and enroll as a student at a private academy.

It was no secret that Belva's father did not think a girl needed an education. Even so, Belva was not timid about asking for his help. She had given him all of her teaching wages, so she needed his financial support to enroll. But Lewis Bennett scoffed at this wild idea and repeatedly said no. Sometimes, to shame her for wanting something more than what he called a "woman's proper place," he would quote the Bible to support his views. A son with Belva's ambitions would have made Lewis Bennett proud, but Belva learned that her dreams embarrassed—even angered—her family.

CHAPTER TWO

WIFE

Belva slowly began to give up her dreams. She accepted the realities of being the daughter of a poor farmer who could not afford to pay private school fees and who did not believe that a girl needed more than a few years of education. In spite of her ambition, it looked as though Belva Bennett was going to have the same life as her mother.

And so, after several years of teaching, eighteen-year-old Belva did what was expected of her. She married her neighbor, Uriah McNall, a twenty-two-year-old farmer. She said, it was "the one avenue open to me." Uriah's family had more money than hers. Belva thought he would make a good, hardworking husband. They married in her parents' little house with relatives smiling at them. Hannah and Lewis were relieved that Belva had come to her senses and realized she could not go to college. As a gift, they gave the newly married couple a large Bible. Belva immediately wrote the date of her wedding in it.

Uriah McNall farmed and ran a sawmill business. His young wife called herself a "helpmate and a true companion." She kept house, much as her mother did. But because math and good business sense came easily to her, Belva was also able to help Uriah with the business. She learned how to joke and gossip as a way of bargaining with the lumbermen who sold the trees to be cut into lumber. She got them to agree to low prices, and she entered the figures in long columns in the sawmill account books. She and Uriah prospered. A year into their marriage, they were delighted when their daughter, Lura, was born.

Things were going well, but Belva was not fully content. Now that she was a married woman, she worried about losing her "individual identity." She fretted that neighbors would expect her to think like

The lumber industry was booming in the 1800s when Belva and her new husband ran a sawmill business in upstate New York. Lumberjacks floated logs downriver from where trees were cut. Logs entered sawmills, where they were turned into sawn boards. French artist Jacques Gérard Milbert painted this sawmill on the Hudson River in eastern New York in the early 1800s.

Uriah, to hold his religious and political views, and to have no ideas of her own. She knew that whatever Uriah might think about her, the law regarded her husband as her superior, not her equal partner. Uriah could vote, and she could not. If he wanted, Uriah could take any money that she earned. She hoped like fury that her marriage was special. She hoped that Uriah would have the spirit to defend a wife who was not afraid to say what she thought.

Shortly after Lura's birth, an accident at the sawmill badly injured Uriah. As a result, he could no longer work. Belva had to take over. Before the accident, she had spent long days cooking, sewing, and growing vegetables. She cared for baby Lura. Standing at the washboard, she scrubbed Lura's cloth diapers until they were clean. After the accident, Belva's days were even longer. She looked after the house and baby, cared for Uriah, and ran the business.

She worked like this for three years, hoping that Uriah would get better. Despite her prayers, Belva's young husband died in 1853, weakened by his accident and lung disease. Little Lura was just turning three.

Suddenly, the question of whether Belva was satisfied with married life no longer mattered. She was a twenty-two-year-old widow with a young daughter to take care of.

Belva never wanted a life like her mother's. With Uriah dead, she was the head of her household with no husband telling her what to do. But life had become a nightmare of work and despair. "I feel hopeless and aimless," she told her family.

Perhaps for this reason, her long-banished dreams returned. Once again, Belva began thinking about college and how it might change her life. With more education, she could make something of herself and take care of Lura without worrying about money. Belva knew that most people thought her dream was silly or even dangerous. Some men and even women believed that women's brains were not capable of deep thinking. Some people were convinced that too much reading and writing could cause poor health.

Always stubborn and now a little desperate, Belva pushed ahead with her new plans. Her friends and family were shocked. One friend asked, "What did she expect to make of [herself]?" They also asked who would look after Lura if Belva went to live in a college dormitory.

In spite of the opposition, Belva was determined to return to school. She called this decision "taking destiny into my hands."

She enrolled as a student at the nearby Gasport Academy. Just standing outside the small brick building and looking at it gave Belva pleasure. Here she would brush up on subjects she had not learned well enough. To support her little family, she found a small house where she and Lura could live while she rented out rooms and cooked her boarders' meals. In this boardinghouse, she juggled the role of mother, innkeeper, and student. She was always busy. Often she could only complete her class assignments late at night, by the light of her new oil lamp.

After finishing her studies at this school, Belva moved to the next step in her plan. In order to go to college, she would have to earn money to pay tuition and living fees. She applied for her old job as a district teacher and was hired. Each day she took Lura to work with her. Lura was five years old and a favorite of the students. Belva taught the younger children their ABCs and struggled to make the older ones understand long division. She loved poetry, and when possible, she would quiet everyone by reading a favorite poem. She taught for more than a year before she had enough money to apply to college.

As a widow with a job, Belva had more freedom than a married woman. No one told her how to use her salary or the property she inherited from Uriah. She could choose where to live, and she could even experiment in becoming someone besides a farmwife. If she was accepted at college, she could use her savings to pay for it. She could not, however, take Lura with her.

Belva didn't want to do anything to harm her daughter and considered giving up her dream of college. Finally, she hit on a solution. Perhaps Lura could live with her grandmother while Belva went to college. Living apart would be difficult, but in the long run, this sacrifice would give them a better life. Belva would be able to get a good job. She hoped Lura would be proud of a mother who had dared to dream of a better life for them.

Hannah listened carefully to Belva's plan. Years before, she had not been willing to help Belva.

This time she sympathized with her daughter's ambitions. Lura would live with her grandmother while Belva studied at Genesee College. Genesee, a school sixty miles away, had just started to accept women students. Lewis Bennett was not as easily convinced. He called Belva's plan unwomanly, but in the end, he agreed. It was the first time he supported Belva's ambitions. Perhaps the fact that she was a widow who needed to support her child finally changed his mind.

With mixed emotions, Belva took the creaky stagecoach to Genesee College in Lima, New York. She was anxious and worried. She wanted to finish her studies as quickly as possible in order to return home to her daughter.

The coach traveled through forests and alongside rolling green pastures. It was Belva's first real journey. She passed close to Seneca Falls, New York. A few years earlier, in 1848, women and men with daring ideas about women's equality had met there. They had published a Declaration of Sentiments. They had modeled this long letter on the Declaration of Independence. Reformers Lucretia Mott, Elizabeth Cady Stanton, Frederick Douglass, and nearly one hundred others said in the declaration that it was time for the unequal treatment of women to stop. They argued that in a democratic society, women should be allowed to vote and have equal rights within marriage, especially control of their property and wages. Like Belva, they insisted that girls should be educated and paid fairly.

Elizabeth Cady Stanton reads the Declaration of Sentiments in 1848 during the Seneca Falls Convention. Other prominent women's rights advocates attended the conference.

Belva knew about the 1848 Declaration of Sentiments. She took comfort knowing she was not alone in thinking that women deserved equal rights.

At Genesee College, Belva wanted to prove that a woman who studied hard could do as well as a man. Members of the Methodist Church had established the college. The recently built College Hall was a handsome redbrick building with tall, imposing columns. It made Lima a popular place for young people wanting an education. A large high school, Genesee Wesleyan Seminary, sat on the same pretty hillside.

On the day Belva walked from the stagecoach stop to the campus, more than one thousand students attended the seminary and the college. Belva saw strangers and activity everywhere. It was quite a change for a young woman who knew everyone back home. Years later, in a speech celebrating the school's fiftieth anniversary, Belva praised the faculty and the church for opening the college to women and giving farm girls like her a chance to improve their lives.

The teachers at Genesee encouraged students to be serious and work hard. With Lura far away and a very limited bank account, Belva had no trouble focusing completely on her studies. She needed to graduate as soon as possible. Belva took courses in politics, history, and science. She worked hard but was lonely living far away from Lura and her parents.

In 1831 the Genesee Wesleyan Seminary was opened in Lima, New York, by the members of the Methodist Church. In 1849 the seminary expanded to become Genesee College, where Belva attended school. College Hall is shown above in this postcard from 1910.

Belva had plenty of quiet thinking time at Genesee. She decided she wanted to serve her country. Because many male leaders were lawyers, Belva started to imagine something incredible for a woman. She would become a lawyer. Full of confidence, she joined several male Genesee students who were attending the private lectures of a young law professor in the village of Lima.

Belva was curious about how the law shaped people's lives. She began to see that the laws of her country helped some people, white men, for example, while enslaving others. She hoped to find a way for the law to make the world a better and fairer place.

In 1856, when Belva attended these law lectures, there was not a single woman lawyer in the United States. Belva needed to earn a living for herself and Lura. It seemed foolish even to think about trying to enter a profession that did not admit women.

But college had once seemed outside of her grasp, and yet here she was at Genesee. She thought maybe she could also open up the profession of law to women. New dreams began to take shape in Belva's mind as she walked from the campus to the building in town where the lectures were held. Belva knew these dreams would take time and patience to achieve.

One night Belva walked into town to hear a talk by women's rights crusader Susan B. Anthony. Like Belva, Anthony thought that people should change their ways and make room for women. Anthony's progressive views made many people angry. One well-known minister accused Susan B. Anthony of being an unfaithful Christian. He called her an infidel, or unbeliever. Belva, however, liked what Anthony said. Her words helped Belva to believe that she could become a lawyer.

The night that Belva went to hear her, Anthony argued that women should be permitted to work in shops and stores, and even in dirty printing offices. She said that men should stop being afraid of competing for jobs with women. As Belva dreamed about someday running her own law office, she thought Anthony was right.

Women seeking equal rights were often portrayed negatively in the media. In this political cartoon that ran on the cover of the New York *Daily Graphic* in 1873, Susan B. Anthony is dressed like a man, wearing a top hat and spurs. Other traditional gender roles in the cartoon are equally distorted, such as a woman police officer, a man holding a baby, and a man holding a shopping basket. In the background, a crowd of women campaign for equality. Belva hoped to break traditional gender roles herself by becoming a lawyer.

Belva graduated from Genesee College in June 1857 and was immediately offered a good teaching job. Although she had "formed other plans," ones she never revealed, her college president told her to accept the position, and she did. The large school was located in Lockport, New York. Lockport was an important and prosperous town on the Erie Canal, near her childhood home.

The new job permitted Belva to live again with Lura, who was now seven years old. At first, Lura was shy with her mother. Both she and Belva were grateful that Aunt Inverno, Belva's younger sister,

This photograph, taken in the late 1800s, shows a view along Main Street in Lockport, New York, where Belva taught school after graduating from Genesee College.

had agreed to come live with them. Inverno had become a big sister to Lura during Belva's absence. She knew what the child liked and didn't like. That was comforting to Lura, as well as to her mother.

Belva supported the small family on her teacher's salary. The three of them set up house in Esther Comstock's boardinghouse. They rented a bedroom from her and ate their meals with the other boarders at the large, noisy dining room table.

Belva was responsible for the financial support of them all. But Lockport was no different from her old district school. Again, she learned that her salary was lower than that of the male teachers. She explained her family responsibilities to the school board and appealed the low pay. But they refused to make any changes. This made her angry and more convinced than ever that she must speak out in public about injustice.

As it happened, many Lockport women had already been meeting to talk about how they could make their community a better place to live. Some of them had formed a Sabbath Society to stop people from doing business on Sunday. They said that people ought to be in church or at rest on Sunday. Other people meeting as a Temperance Society argued that it would be better for families and better for the town if men drank no alcohol. These women were optimistic. They believed that by talking to friends and family about these issues, their town and the towns around them could improve.

The Lockport women were pleased to have the new schoolteacher join in their efforts. But Belva upset them with her strong views about women deserving better treatment. For most of them, the idea of women having rights equal to men was far too controversial. They had been taught that their place was at home and at church, and they were comfortable with that idea. They felt that women ruled through their hearts, while men used their brains.

Belva believed that women were every bit as able as men of making good use of their minds. When an opportunity presented itself to test this belief, Belva jumped at the chance.

At a convention of New York State teachers, Belva again ran into Susan B. Anthony. Every year, Anthony became better known as an outspoken advocate of women's rights. Once a teacher, she stirred up trouble at meetings like these by urging women instructors to fight for better pay and better promotions. This year, in a speech written with her friend Elizabeth Cady Stanton, Anthony set off fireworks with the argument that women were equal in nature and ability to men. She challenged the teachers to give girls an education "equal and identical" and "side by side" to boys.

Cranky male delegates tried to shout her down, but Anthony finished her talk. Belva admired the way she spoke, with a straight back and without fear. When Anthony completed her speech, Belva walked up to the stage. She introduced herself and told Anthony that she also considered it wrong that girls were not required to take the same courses as boys. Classes for boys emphasized mental abilities. Classes for girls

In the 1800s, girls in the United States learned the art of embroidery in school, as well as reading, writing, and arithmetic.

stressed domestic arts such as sewing, cooking, and walking and speaking nicely.

The two women liked each other. Together they decided to test their ideas. Belva would go back to her school and ask the principal if she could conduct an experiment. He agreed. Next, she asked her students, all girls, who would be willing to try something new. Belva would teach these girls a "boy's" subject to see if they could learn it.

The class was public speaking, a course normally only offered to boys. Belva gathered the girls and taught them to write and speak for an audience. Each week they had to give a talk. At first, the girls were terrified. But they practiced and they improved. In the end, they did as well as the boys. Belva and Susan B.

Anthony were thrilled when the school board agreed that public speaking would become a required course for both boys and girls. Later in life, when she became a lawyer, Belva said she would have been better at arguing in court if she had been permitted to take a public speaking class as a girl.

In 1861, after teaching four years in Lockport, Belva decided to move on. Her sister Inverno had graduated from high school and gone home to live with their parents, who were now farming in Illinois. The Northern states and Southern states declared war against each other that year. One of the United States' darkest moments was unfolding as the nation fought the Civil War (1861–1865) over whether it would split and whether it would outlaw slavery. Many people in the North felt that slavery mocked the words "All men are created equal."

Belva and Lura, now a dark-eyed girl of eleven, did not follow Inverno home. Instead, determined to be independent, Belva moved the two of them to the small New York town of Gainesville. Belva took charge of a school for girls there. For the third time in her young life, Lura had to adjust to a new place, away from people she knew and loved.

A few months after they arrived in Gainesville, the school's owner charged Belva with being "immodest and irreligious." She loved athletics and had taken her girl students out for exercise on a frozen pond. (Belva later wrote "the roller-skate and the skating-rink had not then been dreamed of.") The owner banned such outings. Shortly after that, the school building burned to the ground, putting Belva out of work.

Belva took Lura to a school in another small New York town and then to the larger town of Owego, New York. Belva became the owner of a small school there. Lura became one of her pupils at the little brick building, which faced the busy Susquehanna River. Belva taught classes while praying for a Northern Union victory over the Southern Confederacy in the bloody Civil War that was raging. She was eager for the war to end. The conflict deeply troubled her. She believed that people should work out their differences without sending soldiers to fight. She was, however, dedicated to the Union cause. She organized the women of the town in making cloth bandages to send to the battlefront.

When the long war ended in 1865, Belva was restless. Like many people, she saw the victory of the North as a sign for her to make a new beginning. In the winter of 1866, she enrolled Lura, just sixteen, at Genesee Wesleyan Seminary, across from the college she had attended. She bought herself a ticket for Washington, D.C. The nation's capital was the home of great men. Earlier, she had tested the girls in her class to see if they could handle a boy's course. Now, all alone, she was ready to test herself. She wanted to be a leader. She wanted to find a place for herself among the people who made the laws of the nation.

Belva sat for this photographic portrait after arriving in Washington, D.C., in 1866.

CHAPTER THREE

NEWCOMER

Nobody took notice of Belva on the crowded downtown streets of Washington, D.C. Although she was usually a social person, this did not alarm her. There would be time to make friends. She was excited just to be in the nation's capital. As she walked along Pennsylvania Avenue, one of the city's biggest streets, Belva thought about what she needed to do and what she wanted to do. She bought a newspaper and read the job ads. She needed to get a job to pay her expenses while she planned her future and figured out when Lura might join her. Holding her newspaper, she looked up the avenue toward the Capitol building, where members of Congress debated how to govern the nation. Those were the people she wanted to meet, but that would have to wait.

The Washington that Belva saw when she first arrived was not a city that would make anyone proud. Cheap and dingy stores, saloons, and hotels lined the main streets, including Pennsylvania Avenue. Men wounded in the war and freed slaves lived in crowded, dirty conditions. Sometimes, without anywhere to live, they had to camp out on sidewalks. One famous newspaperman observed that some parts of the year, the street was deep mud, but in hot weather, the dust was disgusting. The author Mark Twain joked that the half-finished Washington Monument looked like "a factory chimney with the top broken off."

Even the majestic Capitol, built for meetings of the Congress and the Supreme Court, was not complete. Its handsome dome with the Statue of Freedom had been lifted into place. But when Belva arrived, the additions on each side of the main building were still under construction.

The city was shabby, but most people came to love Washington. Belva certainly did. She had a burning desire to find out what "the great men and women of the country felt and thought." She did not come to see sights or to be a social butterfly. She came to learn how the national government works and to try to become a part of it.

With her grand ambitions, Belva could have used a friend in the government. She needed such a mentor to teach her the ropes, introduce her to the right people, and help her find a good job. She was, after all, a college graduate. Very few men had that much education. But women did not have mentors, so Belva was on her own. She wanted to work for the government, but this was unthinkable for a woman at the time. During the Civil War, a few women had been hired as low-level clerks so men could fight the war. But the idea of a woman, even an educated woman like Belva, becoming a diplomat or an assistant to a member of Congress was just plain laughable.

It was laughable to everyone but Belva. She knew that ambitious men from modest backgrounds like

hers did get these jobs. She was determined to succeed. She was determined that being a woman would
not stand in her way. Through a newspaper ad, she
found a teaching job at a small downtown school. It
did not pay well, but she was done by lunchtime. This
left her free in the afternoons to explore the city she
now called home.

One of Belva favorite walks was the trek up the hill
to the Capitol, where she would spend time sitting in
the Ladies Gallery. From her seat, she listened to the
members of Congress debate laws. These men argued
with one another, often in raised voices, about how

Women could listen
to congressional de-
bate from the Ladies
Gallery, a balcony
overlooking the Senate
floor. This illustration
was made in 1891 by
artist W. T. Smedley.

to help the newly freed slaves. They also debated whether a larger navy was necessary for the protection of the nation and how much to pay the soldiers injured in the Civil War who no longer could work. Belva was fascinated by these men who had been elected to speak their minds in public.

A few months after coming to Washington, Belva decided she had nothing to lose by trying to get a government job. She applied for the job of American consul in Belgium. As a consul, she would assist U.S. citizens visiting Belgium. Hoping for a job interview, she spent hours at the Supreme Court Library reading about international law. Then she waited.

To Belva's "disappointment and chagrin," nobody even acknowledged her application. She was, she later wrote, "too weak-kneed to renew it."

Belva had fallen flat on her face in her first attempt. Fortunately, she had been making friends with other reformers since coming to Washington. These men and women struggled for their causes. They did not think that one failure was anything to cry about. They were people who had strong views about fairness and justice, like Belva.

Many of these reformers were unconventional women. Their accomplishments were remarkable for the mid-1800s. Julia Archibald Holmes had daringly climbed Pike's Peak in the Rocky Mountains. She ran a printing business with her husband. Many people thought she ought to be at home, not dirtying her fingers with printer's ink. Doctors Susan Edson and Mary Walker had fought their way into

Doctor Mary Walker is pictured here in 1866 wearing the Congressional Medal of Honor she earned serving as a surgeon during the Civil War. She belonged to the group of Washington women who strove to break the traditional mold of what was expected of them.

the medical profession. (Some Americans thought it was all right for women doctors to treat women, but that it was indecent for a lady doctor to treat a male patient.) Sara Spencer headed the women's department of her family's business college. She thought it was wrong to be asked to pay taxes but not to be permitted to vote. Josephine Griffing had made a name for herself speaking out against slavery. She was a respected figure in the National Freedman's Relief Association, an aid and education society created to help former slaves. Journalist Emily Briggs wrote about corrupt Washington politics using the feminine pen name Olivia.

These women befriended Belva and gave her their insiders' knowledge of the capital. They were not politicians, but they worked to influence the men who wrote the laws of the nation. These women encouraged Belva's ambitious nature. With their support and encouragement, she began to remake her life.

First, Belva quit her teaching job. She rented a downtown building called the Union League Hall. To make money, she leased some of the space as meeting rooms. Then she turned the rest of the building into a school of her own with an apartment to live in. Soon Lura joined her. Lura was seventeen and had just graduated from the Genesee Seminary. Her mother asked her to teach French and Latin at the school.

Belva's daughter, Lura McNall, joined her mother in Washington, D.C., after graduating from Genesee Seminary.

For some people, running a home and a school, acting as a rental agent, and working for women's rights and other reform causes would leave time for nothing else. Belva, however, had boundless energy. After spending so much time with her bold new Washington friends, Belva was certain that she could become a lawyer. For most of the nineteenth century, lawyers had trained in the offices of older attorneys. Learning this way, as an apprentice, was far more common than attending one of the few law schools.

Belva wanted to "read law" as an apprentice, but no male attorney in Washington was brave enough to take in a woman. Frustrated but not defeated, she bought an old copy of William Blackstone's *Commentaries on the Laws of England*. This important eighteenth-century book explained the laws of Great Britain. It

William Blackstone (1723–1780) wrote *Commentaries on the Laws of England*. The four-volume work was published in the 1760s in Great Britain.

was a kind of legal bible. All students of law (even those in the United States) studied it. Usually, an experienced lawyer guided these apprentice students. Having no guide, Belva would read her law books by lamplight at night when her work as a teacher was over. She gave herself "daily tasks until [she] had read and re-read them through."

Belva also began to court, as dating was then called. She was thirty-seven, smart, and good looking. It had been fifteen years since her husband died. More than one Washington man may have wooed her, but in March 1868 she decided to marry the Reverend Ezekiel Lockwood. He was a dentist and lay preacher (a preacher without religious training), a local man in his late sixties.

The couple married in the building where Lockwood and Lura lived. They invited their friends to the short wedding ceremony, followed by an evening of food and music. Lockwood and her husband were both serious people. Ezekiel, a widower, was a hardworking man. He had just begun a new business as a claims agent. He helped people living in other parts of the country who believed that the government owed them wages or money for property damaged in the Civil War. He was not a lawyer, but he knew a great deal about the law. Lockwood welcomed the idea of his companionship.

As a new wife, Lockwood made jokes to her friends about her decision to marry. Maybe she was worried that they would tease her. After all, she had taken care of herself and Lura for a long time. But she wanted to get ahead and to have more money, not that Ezekiel was particularly well off. Still, she and her husband decided that, for a little while, what he earned would cover their expenses. He agreed that she should close her school and study her law books.

Lockwood was more determined than ever to become one of the first women lawyers in the country. Law had been a stepping-stone to greatness for many men. Why not for her? She continued to think about how the law could be used to win women the right to vote or to control their wages.

Lockwood used nearly all of her spare time to study law. She studied like a demon, driven to prove that women, if only given the opportunity, could succeed at men's work.

In the first year of Lockwood and Ezekiel's marriage, Lockwood also became involved in the fight for women's right to vote in the local Washington elections. She and her friends did not think that the United States deserved to call itself a democracy as long as women, particularly those living in the nation's capital, were kept from the ballot box. Lockwood wanted to vote. She helped organize Washington's Universal Franchise Association (UFA) to make it happen as quickly as possible.

At UFA meetings, speakers explained why it was unfair to deny women the right to vote. Announcements in local newspapers spread the word about these meetings. That was when the trouble began. Many men were outraged by these suffragist women. They believed that only men should speak and vote for their families. They felt that politics was a dirty business where cigar-smoking politicians made backroom deals. No lady should have anything to do with voting and politics. If she did, that was proof that she was not a true lady. She was, rather, a loud, bossy woman whose husband could not keep her in her place.

Wanting to show off and to embarrass women like Lockwood, rowdy opponents of suffrage came to the meetings. These hecklers shouted at the speakers and tried to silence them by hissing and booing. Sometimes even the police (all men), who were called in to help, would let the hecklers continue. A young family friend of Lockwood's remembered a night when these bullies threw rotten vegetables and rolled metal plates among the chairs to make noise. He thought Lockwood and her friends had incredibly "strong spirits which ridicule could not swerve."

Within the first year of her marriage, Lockwood learned that she was pregnant. In her day, proper ladies did not appear in public in the later months of pregnancy. Lockwood thought this custom was old-fashioned and ridiculous. People might think that her behavior was scandalous, but she refused to stay away from her reform meetings. She even spoke at some of them. At home she continued to pore over her law books. She told her husband, Lura, and her friends that she had a "mania for the law" that nothing could cure.

In late January 1869, Jessie Belva Lockwood was born. The Lockwoods and nineteen-year-old Lura turned their attention to the much-loved baby girl. Lockwood called her "my little blossom." She wrote that Jessie awakened her deep motherly love, but she was clear that the baby would not stop her from working hard for reform causes.

Jessie's birth did not put a stop to her mother's mania for the law either. Lockwood continued to think that she could become an attorney, even with a baby to look after. She might as well have said that she intended to be an army general or the nation's president. Most people thought that a lady in a court of law—sitting near dangerous criminals and men spitting chewing tobacco—was not proper. It was fine to be a teacher or even a woman doctor taking care of other women, but not a lawyer.

Lockwood had never cared much about doing what was expected of her. So in October 1869, challenging what most people thought was right and proper, she applied to become a student at a law school in Washington, D.C.

When she asked to enroll in the law department of the Columbian College, Lockwood probably knew that two young women had just been accepted at a Saint Louis, Missouri, law school. She quickly found out, however, that in the eastern part of the United States, where she lived, people were less willing to change old ways of doing things. A short time after applying to Columbian, she received a letter from the school president. He wrote that she would not be admitted. Her presence, a woman's presence, in class "would be likely to distract the attention of the young men."

This letter was a disappointment. But standing with baby Jessie on her hip, Lockwood also thought it was funny that these men imagined that a middle-aged mother, sitting at a desk, would be disruptive.

Fortunately, there were many things to distract Lockwood from this disappointment. In January 1870, a new group of reform women, calling themselves the National Woman Suffrage Association, held a big meeting in Washington near her home. The respected Elizabeth Cady Stanton spoke on the first day. She won thunderous applause when she predicted that all American women would shortly be granted the right to vote. (Oh, how wrong she was!) Other women talked about the need to take action.

The idea of taking action appealed to Lockwood. In spite of her recent law school rejection, she was hopeful about the movement for women's rights. She

Members of the National Woman Suffrage Assocation, including Susan B. Anthony and Elizabeth Cady Stanton, sought out new members to join the group of reformers. This image from the 1870s shows one of their meetings.

knew that she was part of something important.

Congress had recently refused to improve the salaries of women government workers. As a teenager and again in Lockport, Lockwood had vowed to fight this kind of unfairness and discrimination. She knew firsthand how much it hurt to do the same job as a man but to be paid less. In the spring of 1870, she started a campaign to push members of Congress to vote for higher salaries for the government's women employees.

She wrote down her ideas and took them to Samuel Arnell, a Tennessee congressman concerned with the problems workers faced. She asked him to introduce legislation to ensure that women who wanted to work for the U.S. government would be treated fairly. He agreed, and in March of that year, his proposal was introduced to Congress. If approved, it would become a law. It was called "A bill to do justice to the female employees of the Government." It asked that a woman be given the same right as a man to take hiring examinations and, if hired, be paid the same as any man doing that job.

The Arnell bill caused an uproar. Most of the members of Congress, all men, did not care about gender discrimination. They had no sympathy for women who had to work. They were even less concerned about whether women could compete for government jobs. But a few brave congressmen agreed with Arnell's bill. Arnell and these men insisted that the proposal be debated.

Some opponents of the bill argued that the government could not afford to pay women a fair wage. They said that the only reason to hire women was because the government saved money by hiring them instead of men. Arnell argued that paying women a small wage was unjust and undervalued them as human beings.

When the members of Congress finally voted, they approved a version of the legislation Lockwood had written for Arnell. It wasn't as strong as Lockwood's original idea, but it was a victory nonetheless. Lockwood was thrilled about the new law that would help women, even though she knew it did not do nearly enough.

The process taught Lockwood how to talk to members of Congress and how to persuade them to alter their views. After months of talking and listening, Lockwood began to understand this art of lobbying, the methods citizens use to convince elected officials to vote for particular laws.

CHAPTER FOUR

LAWYER

Heavy, hot humidity often fell on Washington during the summer. The weather seemed to help bring on disease. But no one understood what caused many of the illnesses that struck residents of the city. Whooping cough, measles, scarlet fever, cholera, and typhoid fever threatened Washington families, including the Lockwoods.

Late in the summer of 1870, Jessie, almost two years old, became ill. Lockwood had been busy with the Arnell bill and lobbying for women's right to vote. Lura had begun a new job at a book bindery. Ezekiel, too, had been caught up with work. But they all stopped what they were doing to care for Jessie. The baby developed a high fever and stopped eating. Her stomach hurt, and she was tired and listless. Her parents pressed cool washcloths on her hot skin, but nothing brought her fever down. The Lockwoods became increasingly worried. Jessie was precious to them. Lockwood suspected that Jessie had typhoid fever, a disease caused by unclean food and water. The three adults watched over the toddler day and night. But they were not able to save her.

Jessie's death was a great blow to the family. Lockwood had always said that Jessie was a "great comfort and blessing." Now she had to face life without her little girl. She was deeply affected. Usually very public and outspoken, Lockwood became quiet and kept to herself. With Lura and husband by her side, she closed her apartment door and, for a while, closed out the world.

Lockwood, a fighter by nature, was finally able to push back her darkest thoughts. She resolved to honor Jessie's memory by working for laws to protect children from parents who hurt them. Still mourning, she threw herself into a campaign to prohibit the sale of alcohol. She believed that many parents harmed their children after drinking too much.

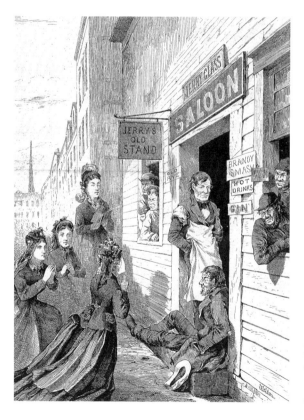

In 1874 temperance crusaders protest the sale of liquor outside a local saloon.

Her friends and this new cause helped lift Lockwood's spirits. She slowly regained her strength and spirit. She began to think about what she would do in the months and years ahead.

Cold, hard reality determined part of the answer. Lockwood was forty years old, and her husband was in his late sixties. She could help him with his government claims business, but there was no denying that in a few years, Lockwood would have to support the household. And so, six months after Jessie's death, Lockwood again applied to law school. This time, amazingly, she was accepted at the National University Law School in Washington, D.C.

Lockwood thought that the school decided to admit women because it was new and needed students. Whatever the reason, she seized the chance to enroll. Several other Washington women also signed up. They were ladies, Lockwood said, who registered primarily "as a novelty" and without any idea about how hard they would have to study.

The women had been told that the classes would be coeducational, with women and men studying the law together. When they arrived at the school, however, they were taken to a separate room. The women were shocked and insulted. Lockwood explained to friends that the men "had set up a growl," insisting that they would not sit in a classroom with women. They said women were inferior. Lockwood wondered if they were just afraid of competing with women or being shown up by them.

The angry reaction of the men and the unwelcoming

environment of the school were difficult to deal with. Most of the female students dropped out. Even Lura, who had attended class with her mother for a few months, left the program. But Lockwood and Lydia Hall, a government clerk, refused to quit even though they found sitting in a separate classroom humiliating. They studied summer and winter. Lockwood was happy that she had spent all those months, years before, reading important law books. It was preparation that served her well and made her a better student. As she sat reading her heavy books at home, Jokes, her little bird, sometimes sang away in his cage near her.

As graduation approached, Lockwood and Hall made plans to sit on the school's stage and be presented to Washington's legal community as new lawyers. Lockwood was excited about graduating. If becoming a lawyer was a stepping-stone, she was on her way to good things. But in the weeks before the ceremony, she and Lydia Hall were suddenly told that they had not studied long enough. They would not receive their diplomas, and they would not be permitted to sit on the stage with the men.

The women were devastated. They had worked hard and passed their courses. They wanted their diplomas. They were determined to show that women were just as good as men at using their brains.

They had another reason they wanted to graduate with the men. The graduating members of a law class were presented together to become members of the local bar association. Membership in the bar association required a good knowledge of the law and excellent moral character. Being accepted into this group was recognition that would bring business to a lawyer and permit him (or her) to argue a case in any local court.

The officials of the law school said their decision was final. Lockwood and Hall were furious. They did not give up. They asked for a chance to prove their knowledge of the law through an extra, oral examination. A special bar examination committee was set up. Each woman sat for two long days answering questions. They did well. But the members of the bar association secretly had decided not to admit them, no matter how well they answered.

Lydia Hall finally gave up. She got married and moved away. Lockwood, however, refused to have her ambitions squelched. She had fought hard her whole life and had proved that she would move forward and not let anyone stand in her way. Lockwood was a mature woman. She'd lost a husband and a baby. She had been treated unfairly by employers, educators, and her peers for as long as she could remember. She was not about to give up her dreams.

Lawyer friends arranged for her to take another oral examination. This one went on and on and on—three days of questioning. At the end, the examiners refused to make a report on her answers. She was fed up and called them "culprits" who did not want the world to change. To her, they were as guilty as any criminal.

Most people would have quit. Lockwood did feel discouraged and did not want to look foolish. But she was determined to open a law practice, and she couldn't do this without being admitted to the bar.

In the summer of 1872, Lockwood went to the southern United States for three months to clear her head. She also earned a little money as a journalist writing for a New York City newspaper called the *Golden Age.* The paper's owner supported the presidential candidacy of Horace Greeley, so Lockwood also agreed to campaign for him. Greeley was not a strong champion of women's rights, but Lockwood liked his other ideas. She particularly liked his belief that since the Civil War had been over for seven years, it was time for the former enemies to work together to end old hatreds.

Lura had also started to write a newspaper column. Hers was about life and politics in Washington. She

Horace Greeley *(left)* was the founder and editor of the *New York Tribune.* He ran for U.S. president in 1872 but lost the race to Civil War hero Ulysses S. Grant. Lockwood supported many of Greeley's stances and campaigned for him.

had a sharp tongue and did not mind tossing a little gossip into her articles. Lura adored her mother and admired her daring.

Returning from the South, Lockwood decided to continue the fight for her law diploma. She thought that if she signed up for more classes, the university would give her a diploma. She asked officials to read-mit her, but they refused. She commented to friends and family that since first accepting her as a student, National University had "shut up like an oyster." No one at the school wanted women to become lawyers. When she learned their final decision, Lockwood felt that she had no choice but to write to the president of the United States.

President Ulysses S. Grant was partly respon-sible for the things that happened at the National University. He was its honorary president. In early September 1873, Lockwood wrote to him. In a long letter, she explained that the university had enrolled her in its law program and she had been a serious student. She told Grant that she wanted to earn her living as an attorney and that it was an injustice to be denied the diploma just because she was a woman.

She put her letter in the mail. A few hours later, she decided that her words had not been forceful enough. So she wrote a second, much less polite letter:

Sir, —You are, or you are not, President of the National University Law School. If you are its President, I desire to say to you that I have passed through the curriculum of study in this school, and am entitled to, and demand my diploma.

>Very respectfully,
>Belva A. Lockwood

Lockwood never heard from President Grant, but two weeks later, the head of the university presented her with the long-denied diploma. A week later, on September 24, 1873, she was admitted to the District of Columbia bar association. She became the second woman attorney in the capital—a few months before, a Howard Law School graduate, Charlotte E. Ray, had become the first.

CHAPTER FIVE

FIGHTER

Lockwood never doubted that she would succeed as a lawyer, even though most Americans thought of law as a man's job. She had even started to help clients in small ways before writing her letters to President Grant. Once she was a full-fledged attorney, Lockwood advertised her services in the newspaper and on business cards. She used the British term for lawyer: Belva A. Lockwood, Solicitor.

People began coming to her small office. Some of her visitors were curious to see what a woman lawyer looked like. Some of her clients were friends and neighbors. None of these people was rich. They were ordinary, working people. They probably hoped that because she was a woman, Lockwood would not charge them much for filing legal papers or representing them in court. She defended men and women accused of crimes such as burglary, forgery, and even murder. She helped women who were divorcing their husbands (often because the men drank too much) and orphans who needed to have a guardian appointed for them. Civil War veterans came to her for help in claiming their military pensions. Women distressed about their ruined reputations rang her doorbell. They hoped to win money in court from men who had promised to marry them but then ran away.

This work interested Lockwood, and she did it well. Lura, now in her twenties, helped with the paperwork. While his health permitted, Ezekiel also lent a hand in the office. But in the winter of 1877, he became increasingly frail and died. Lockwood went into mourning. Ezekiel had been a good husband. He had taught her about filing claims against the government for clients. He supported her fight for equal rights for women and had not complained when people made jokes about a man married to such a stubborn, modern woman. Ezekiel had shared Lockwood's dream of woman suffrage and of women being treated fairly at work. His faith in her ideas made Lockwood even more determined to make these changes occur.

In the summer after Ezekiel's death, Lockwood's success enabled her to buy a four-story house in downtown Washington. It was four years after she had begun working as a lawyer. The house was a row house with buildings on either side. There was nothing fancy about her new home, but it had twenty small rooms. She made the bottom floor into a law office. To earn extra money, she rented out some of the rooms. The rest she kept for her extended family. Lura shared the house with her mother. When Lura married, her husband, DeForest Ormes, joined her there. Lockwood's widowed mother, Hannah, also lived with them. Lockwood adopted one of her nieces, Clara, whose mother had recently died. Clara too lived on F Street. She helped Lura in the office and remained for several years after her marriage.

Several women who had read about Lockwood's success as an attorney signed up as boarders. They wanted to learn the law from her. One of these women, Marilla Ricker, became a lifelong friend. Lockwood and Ricker worked together for many years trying to open new jobs, such as police officer and notary public, to women.

Sometimes the house seemed as if it would burst at the seams. Everyone made an effort to get along, and generally they did. They were proud to live in the house of a woman who fought for equal rights. They were also getting used to reading about her in the newspapers.

Perhaps because she was a fighter and such a practical woman, Lockwood's friends and family were not at all surprised when she became the first woman in Washington, D.C., to ride a bicycle.

Washingtonians who saw Lockwood on this bicycle (actually an adult's tricycle) were shocked. Women, some said, simply did not do such a thing. It was immodest. Her skirt might be blown up by the wind and her stockings and ankles might peek out. Lockwood listened to people's criticism. She thought they were old fogies not willing to change with the times. She had noticed that men with law offices on F Street had bought this new invention and rode bicycles to get around town more quickly. She wanted to compete and be as efficient and successful as the men. If this meant using a bicycle, she was all for it. When the newspapers

This illustration from 1881 shows Lockwood riding a bicycle in public, a daring decision for her time.

Mrs Belva Lockwood.

called her unladylike, she defended herself in a poem.

A simple home woman, who only had thought
To lighten the labors her business had wrought.
And make a machine serve the purpose of feet
And at the same time keep her dress from the
  street.

Lockwood kept riding her bicycle. For many years, though, she was one of the few women brave enough to do so.

****

Some years earlier, Lockwood had started a small war with the government of the United States. The issue was again whether men could deny her, a qualified attorney, the same rights as male lawyers.

Lockwood wanted to represent clients in federal as well as local courts. She was hired to bring a case to the U.S. Court of Claims. She went before the judges and tried to speak on behalf of her client. But the judges told her that a woman—in particular, a married woman—could not work in their courtroom. Their rules only let men argue cases. As a married woman, Lockwood could not do business in her own name (even though she was already doing just that in the local courts).

Vowing to fight these federal judges, Lockwood hired her own lawyer. This attorney argued that the members of the claims court were using old rules. But the judges stubbornly held to their decision. They told Lockwood to take her complaint to the U.S. Supreme Court if she was unhappy.

Lockwood was very unhappy. However, instead of going to the Supreme Court, the highest court in the land, she decided to use her skills as a lobbyist. She thought that Congress should write a law forbidding discrimination against women lawyers.

Some men in the Congress agreed with Lockwood, but not enough to pass a new law. Lockwood had no choice but to go to the Supreme Court. Her friend, lawyer Albert Gallatin Riddle, went with her. They asked the justices to change the rules so that qualified women attorneys could argue cases in federal courts. The nine justices discussed the matter in private. Three of them thought that the time had come to apply the same rules to men and women. But six justices agreed that "women lawyers will only be able to argue in our courts if Congress orders it."

So Lockwood went back to Congress, determined to get the rules changed. She knew people were gossiping about her struggle. At a White House dinner, the wife of one Supreme Court justice told the other guests that "the people of Washington generally were laughing in their sleeves" over Lockwood's efforts.

When Lockwood went back to Congress, she had been crusading for almost three years. She was struggling to keep up her spirits. In the House of Representatives, her cause finally won a yes vote. However, Lockwood then had to convince the more conservative members of the Senate. This was a tougher fight. Many of these men thought that this law

Albert Gallatin Riddle (1816–1902) accompanied Lockwood to the U.S. Supreme Court, where he motioned that she be accepted as a member of its bar. This first attempt was unsuccessful, but Lockwood would not give up.

would be an "entering wedge for woman suffrage." One senator said, "I am not in favor of women voting and this bill may lead to it."

But a majority of senators believed that what Lockwood wanted was right and proper. They pointed out that the world was changing and the Senate ought to change with it. They also noted that men who opposed Lockwood wanted to keep all the good, high-paying jobs.

In the end, Lockwood's supporters won. The new law passed. When President Rutherford B. Hayes signed it, the law became official. It gave all qualified women attorneys the right to practice law in any federal court. Her little war had lasted five years.

On March 3, 1879, dressed in her best black velvet skirt and jacket, Belva Lockwood went back to the Supreme Court. It was a day of great triumph. One New York newspaper reported that a large crowd had come to see Lockwood. When her turn came, she stood with dignity before the justices and was sworn in as the first woman admitted to argue cases before the country's highest court. Friends and family crowded around her, cheering loudly, as the court's marshal called for order. Through her five-year crusade, the lady lawyer from F Street had pushed the reluctant members of Congress to enact one of the first national laws in support of women's rights.

Lockwood wanted the honor of being the first woman lawyer to argue a case at the Supreme Court. More than a year after her swearing in, the chance presented itself. She and attorney Mike L. Woods had

The U.S. Supreme Court awarded Lockwood this certificate when she was admitted to the Court's bar on March 3, 1879.

a client, Caroline Kaiser, whose dispute was going to be heard by the Supreme Court. Lockwood and Woods went to the courtroom and waited their turn to talk. Attorney Woods began to explain the issues as he and Lockwood understood them. Then he stepped aside and let her take over. Attorney Lockwood spoke for twenty minutes. It was the first time in U.S. history that a woman lawyer's voice was heard in legal argument at the Supreme Court. That night Washington's *Evening Star* newspaper put Lockwood on the front page. She had broken another barrier and had showed what women could do if given the chance.

By this time, Lockwood was a celebrity known for her stubborn belief that all people should be treated fairly. She was very happy to be asked to sponsor

Frank Leslie's Illustrated Newspaper ran this illustration of Lockwood *(left)* sponsoring Samuel R. Lowery's admittance to the U.S. Supreme Court bar. Lowery *(second from left, standing)* was the fifth black attorney and the first African American lawyer from the South to receive the honor.

the admission of an African American attorney to practice law before the Supreme Court. Samuel R. Lowery was the first southern African American lawyer seeking this honor. The son of a slave, he was trained as a teacher and scientist as well as an attorney. He and Lockwood stood together before the justices, a sign of change in the United States. One newspaper reporter wrote, "Who dares say the world is not progressing, when, on the motion *of a woman,* a black man is admitted to practice in the highest court of the land?" Nobody commented that Lockwood still could not vote or that the country had a long way to go to end racial discrimination.

Cartoonist E. W. Gustin poked fun at the idea of woman suffrage in this 1909 cartoon. In it, an aproned husband is left behind with a pile of dishes and two crying babies as his wife, wearing a hat and tie, steps out on election day.

CHAPTER SIX

PRESIDENTIAL CANDIDATE

Lockwood's friend Elizabeth Cady Stanton had predicted that women would be granted the right to vote very soon. A change in the U.S. Constitution was all that was needed. She and Lockwood and their pro-suffrage reformer friends campaigned hard for the vote. But many men were afraid to let women vote. They knew it would affect which political party had more power and what laws would pass. To disguise their fears, these men claimed that voting was not ladylike. They also claimed that if women voted, it would destroy family life. Husbands would be "henpecked" by nagging wives, and children would not be properly looked after.

Women in the United States had always been interested in politics and in the well-being of their country. They contributed in many important ways during the American Revolution (1775–1783). When the Constitution was being written, women discussed what ideas should be in it. One Massachusetts patriot, Mercy Otis Warren, suggested that the Constitution needed a Bill of Rights. Later, as political parties developed, women attended rallies and started women's campaign clubs. Before and during the Civil War,

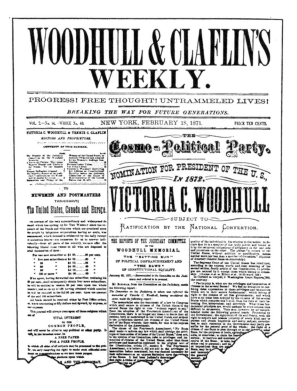

Victoria Woodhull and her sister Tennessee Claflin established the newspaper *Woodhull & Claflin's Weekly*, in which Woodhull announced her presidential candidacy on February 18, 1871. She was the first woman to run for president in the United States. Women still did not have the right to vote.

many women fought for government policies that would end slavery. Elizabeth Cady Stanton announced that she would be happy to become a member of Congress. In 1871 New York City newspaper owner Victoria Woodhull organized a small campaign to run for president of the United States. Of course, neither Stanton nor Woodhull could vote.

In the late summer of 1884, Lockwood decided that she also would run for president. She, too, could not vote. This was exactly the reason that Lockwood said she would be a candidate. She wanted to show Americans that women were interested in politics and could be interesting, intelligent candidates. She wanted to make absolutely clear how wrong it was, in a democracy, to

Twelve years after Victoria Woodhull's unsuccessful bid for U.S. president, Lockwood decided to take her own chance on the campaign trail as the candidate of the Equal Rights Party. The New York *Daily Graphic* printed this etching from a photo of Lockwood on September 11, 1884, with her announcement.

prevent one-half of the population from taking part in elections. She knew that her country would be a better place if all people had an equal chance to speak about the government. Women were citizens and paid taxes. Why shouldn't they vote for the people who represented them? Indeed, why shouldn't they run for office?

Lockwood agreed to run as the candidate of the Equal Rights Party. This political party was made up of a small group of women in California. They thought women ought to gain experience in politics even though they were still voteless. They had no money to give Lockwood to help her advertise her campaign, but Lockwood was a clever and practical woman. Having agreed to be the candidate of the Equal Rights Party, she did everything that a male candidate would do.

On a lovely September day, she held a rally in the village of Wilson's Station, Maryland. It was in the country a few miles outside of Washington, D.C. People could easily travel there by local railroad train. Lockwood's supporters put notices of the meeting and how to get there in the Washington newspapers.

The meeting was at a farmhouse owned by a woman friend. The campaign workers put out picnic tables and brought out food and lemonade. The

Belva Lockwood, photographed in 1884

workers set up stage near the tables. It was decorated with colorful cloth and American flags. Everyone was in a good mood, pleased with the thought that they were helping their country cast off old ways.

Even though they were at a country picnic, Lockwood dressed to make an impression. She wanted to be taken seriously. She wore a proper black silk dress with white lace cuffs. She pinned on her favorite cameo pin, the one showing two horses kicking their legs in the air. Then she walked to the stage where she would speak.

Friends, family, and curious onlookers joined newspaper reporters to hear Lockwood announce that she was a candidate for president. She told her audience that she would travel around the country talking to men and women about what she would do as president. Since George Washington had been elected the first leader of the United States, only men had been president. Lockwood stood before the hundred people gathered at this meeting and said that it was time to let women participate in politics. It was time to let women vote and, yes, even run for president. She told these well-wishers, "I cannot vote, but I can be voted for."

Lockwood held another lively rally at her house on F Street. The parlors were decorated with American flags. At the end of one hall, guests walked under a large canvas poster announcing Lockwood as the presidential candidate of the Equal Rights Party. At this meeting, Lockwood announced to everyone that Lura would be her campaign manager. Her mother, Hannah Bennett, looked on proudly.

Newspaper editors were given a statement that outlined twelve of Lockwood's most important ideas. This was the Equal Rights Party platform. Lockwood proposed equal political rights for all citizens regardless of sex, country of origin, or race. She wanted fair taxes on products brought in from other countries and an international court that would help end war. Not surprisingly, she argued that a woman should be nominated to serve on the U.S. Supreme Court the next time there was a vacancy.

The Equal Rights Party did not have a treasury, and Lockwood was not rich. Still, she wanted to take her campaign to the people of the United States. This was 1884, and the transcontinental railroad was already fifteen years old. Instead of slow, creaky stagecoaches, people were making their way across America on fast trains.

Lockwood loved the idea of using the railroad to travel from her home in Washington, D.C., on the Atlantic coast, to California, on the edge of the Pacific Ocean. She wanted to give political speeches along the way. But she needed money to pay her train fare, so she agreed to give paid lectures anywhere in the country. She gave talks at churches, county fairs, and town halls. Her fees paid the fare on trains that took her from one state to another.

Because this was the first full campaign by a woman, reporters paid attention to what Lockwood said and did. One newspaper published a story about Lockwood having her campaign photograph taken. The reporter said that when she entered the photographer's studio, the owner waved her over to a small chair. Lockwood refused to sit in that chair. She had seen the chair where the other presidential candidates had been posed for their campaign portraits. "Why don't you place me in *that* chair?" she asked.

"That is the Presidential chair," replied the photographer.

"Well, sir," Lockwood answered, "I will sit in that chair. I think I am able to fill it as well as any who have occupied it."

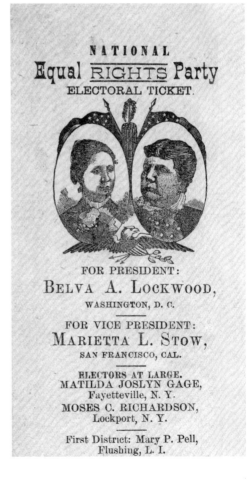

Belva Lockwood and her vice-presidential running mate, Marietta L. Stow, are featured on the 1884 Equal Rights Party ticket.

In this political cartoon from the 1884 presidential election, the out-sider candidates are portrayed as a circus sideshow act. Along with Lockwood *(left, in the ballet dress)*, the other candidates included Benjamin Butler *(center, wearing a B)* of the Greenback Party and John St. John *(right, holding cane)* for the Prohibition Party.

Many Americans thought that it was wrong—or just plain silly—for a voteless woman to run for president. Newspapers ran cartoons about Lockwood's campaign. Sometimes, the artists made fun of her. One cartoonist drew Lockwood campaigning in a ballerina's costume. Lockwood didn't mind the political cartoons. She knew that the newspapers also poked fun at the male candidates. After the election, she told a friend that she was keeping one cartoon as a reminder of the campaign. She said that it was a treasured possession.

Americans were divided about whether a woman should run for president. In the same way, they had different opinions about whether the time had come to let women vote. Lockwood heard all sorts of views when she traveled around the country on her campaign. Although she did not see them, she heard that men had started Belva Lockwood Clubs in a few towns. These fellows paraded on the street wearing large cloth bonnets and Mother Hubbard dresses (long, loose dresses that fell to their ankles). Most people thought the men intended to make fun of Lockwood's campaign. Others thought the parades were meant to make people think about why women were not allowed to vote.

Even Lockwood's women friends did not agree about whether she should be a candidate. Longtime friend Marilla Ricker thought it was a good idea and helped Lockwood campaign for votes. Other members of the

A parade of men wearing Mother Hubbard dresses amuses a crowd in Rahway, New Jersey, in 1884.

women's rights movement were afraid that Lockwood's campaign would give men a new reason to ridicule "those rights women." Susan B. Anthony did not openly criticize Lockwood, but she did not work for her victory either. Lockwood learned an important lesson. Women wanted their rights, but they had different ideas about how to make this happen. Not all women thought the same way. Lockwood also learned to do what she thought was right, as long as she was willing to take the consequences.

One day while Lockwood was away campaigning, the postman brought an envelope for her. A man had written a poem about her:

> O, Belva Ann!
> Fair Belva Ann!
> I know that thou art not a man;
> But I shall vote,
> Pull off my coat,
> And work for thee, fair Belva Ann.

The poem, like the cartoons, amused good-natured Lockwood. She did not know if the man would really campaign for her, but she appreciated that he had taken the time and trouble to write to her. She was also pleased when an important and popular journal, *Frank Leslie's Illustrated Newspaper,* offered her campaign good wishes headed: "Woman in politics. Why not?" And she liked it when a popular magazine described her as a woman with a great deal of determination.

The campaign kept Lockwood busy. She hoped to

get all the candidates together for a debate. She invited the men to join her at an appointed place to talk about political issues. None of the male candidates even showed Lockwood the courtesy of answering her invitation. Perhaps they were not daring enough to appear on a stage with a woman candidate.

The day before the election, Lockwood returned from a campaign tour on the West Coast. She told reporters that she would wait for the election results at her F Street home. They were welcome to come by and visit.

When all the votes were counted, the Democratic Party candidate, Grover Cleveland of New York, was the winner with 46 percent of the popular vote. Lockwood only received about five thousand votes. She was not at all disappointed, however. The campaign had given her the opportunity to teach a huge civics lesson.

Her political campaign showed that she lived in a country where women could speak their minds. She had used that freedom to run a political campaign. She had proven that a woman could discuss politics with intelligence and that people would listen. At least nobody had thrown tomatoes or rotten eggs at her.

After this election, men and women saw that the times were changing. Towns and states began to permit women to vote on certain local political questions—taxes, school board candidates, and the sale of alcohol. By the 1890s, more brave women were running for public office. Not for president—that was still too daring. But they did run for school boards, city councils, and even mayor. It was a start, and Lockwood's campaign had helped to make it happen.

CHAPTER SEVEN

WORLD TRAVELER

Lockwood had accomplished a great deal since moving to Washington, D.C. People all over the country were aware of what she had done. When the presidential campaign ended, she might have continued to practice law. She could still be the famous woman who was always willing to give interviews to newspaper reporters. But Lockwood could not be happy living in the past, talking about what she had already done. She always had new ideas and new plans for improving the world.

While campaigning, Lockwood discovered that she liked traveling. She was good at giving talks, and she decided to work both as a lawyer and a paid lecturer. This was years before the invention of radio, television, or the Internet. It was a time when famous people traveled to small towns, as well as large cities, and gave lectures on entertaining and important subjects.

A man named Henry L. Slayton thought that Lockwood could be quite successful on the lecture circuit. He knew that people were curious to learn more about this women's rights champion. Henry had a business that scheduled lecturers and sent them around the country. Lockwood signed a contract to work for him. She copied her old lectures and wrote new ones. Then she got on a train and began crisscrossing the United

When Lockwood gave public lectures, she was billed as the Great Washington Lawyer. Lyceums (associations providing public lectures) brought lecturers, public programs, and entertainment to many U.S. towns and cities.

States. Slayton sent out advertisements saying he had the honor to announce: "BELVA LOCKWOOD, The Great Washington Lawyer."

Lockwood talked about everything: what she saw during her travels, what she thought about the politicians in Washington, why women should have equal rights, and whether marriage was a good idea. (She said, "Yes, Sir!") Sometimes, she stayed overnight with friends. More often, she stayed at plain hotels. Other lecturers complained about the unheated rooms and poor food, but not Lockwood. She was hardworking and liked to meet new people. Friends seldom heard her grumble about her life.

When she was not on the road giving talks, Lockwood loved being at home at the house on F Street. Lura had learned a lot from Lockwood and helped by being the office manager. Lura's little girl, Inez, loved to play in her grandmother's law office. Lockwood once told a reporter that Inez was a "wonderfully clever child." She didn't mention that Inez sometimes got into mischief and that once she had knocked over a candle, setting the curtains and a few legal papers on fire.

In 1888 the Equal Rights Party again asked Lockwood to be its presidential candidate. She accepted the party's nomination. For the second time, she traveled the country to talk to voters. In New York City, Nellie Bly, the famous "daredeveil girl reporter," interviewed her. Bly wrote a long and flattering article about Lockwood for the *New York World* newspaper. She said that the lady candidate had a good, firm handshake and was smart and lively.

In this campaign, Lockwood raised some new issues. She said that there was enough money in the government's treasury so that some should be used to build new schools. She told voters that girls should be given as good an education as boys and that girls should be prepared to support themselves. That included married women!

Lockwood urged that there be fair policies toward Native Americans. She criticized the poor treatment of Chinese immigrants, many of whom had been brought to the United Stated to help build the railroads. She talked about how the great nations of the world might stop war. She proposed establishing international courts and teaching people the principles of peace. In her 1884 campaign, Lockwood had had a woman running mate, Marietta Stow. This time

In 1888 Lockwood decided to run again for U.S. president with the Equal Rights Party. In this political cartoon, a man *(middle)* is being courted by all the presidential candidates, including Lockwood *(kneeling)*, as they appeal for his vote. In the tight race, Grover Cleveland *(right, rear)* won the popular vote but lost the race to Benjamin Harrison *(left)*, who earned more electoral votes.

Charles Stuart Wells was listed as the vice-presidential candidate of the Equal Rights Party. This made little difference to the voters, however, and again Lockwood lost the election.

After this campaign, Lockwood decided to spend more time on working for world peace. She belonged to the Universal Peace Union. This organization believed that nations did not have to fight when they had disagreements. Its members thought that by using treaties and courts and by teaching the principles of love, justice, and nonviolence to young

Alfred Henry Love helped found the Universal Peace Union (UPU), which launched in 1866 after the end of the Civil War. Lockwood joined the UPU and traveled overseas in support of peace.

people in school, the world could be free of fighting. The Universal Peace Union had a motto: "Remove the causes and abolish the custom of war, establish and live the principles of peace."

A few months after the 1888 election, Lockwood agreed to travel to France to represent the Universal Peace Union at a meeting of people from all over the world who opposed war. This was the first time that she crossed the Atlantic Ocean.

The ship she was to take to Europe was docked in New York City. The night before it sailed, friends gave Lockwood a party to wish her well on her trip. The next day, she boarded the ship with Amanda Deyo, one of the first clergywomen (church officials) in the United States. She was also a member of the Universal Peace Union. On board, the two women studied French and spoke to the other passengers about their peace group. They landed the last week in May in the busy port city of Antwerp, Belgium. Lockwood and Amanda had enjoyed the voyage, but now they were ready to do some sightseeing. In Antwerp they toured a garden known for its flowers and its fruit trees bursting with spring blossoms. Here and at Mainz and Heidelberg in Germany, they walked the city streets and visited well-known cathedrals.

Deyo and Lockwood's meeting was in Paris, the beautiful capital of France. The people of Paris were celebrating the hundredth anniversary of the French Revolution (1789–1799) with an enormous summer-long celebration. An international fair filled many new buildings with exhibits of art, science, and technology. New trees had been planted, and across the Seine River, an amazing thousand-foot structure rose above the city. This was the Eiffel Tower, a marvel of crisscrossing pieces of iron. Lockwood felt very small standing below it.

At the international meeting, Lockwood was introduced to the leaders of the European peace movement. One of them was Frédéric Passy, who would later be the first person to be awarded the Nobel Peace Prize. Lockwood was honored to sit near him on the stage. When it was her turn to make a brief speech, she praised France and called Paris "the city of cities." The next day, Lockwood gave a speech calling for the development of new laws and courts that would discourage war.

After nearly two months in Paris, Lockwood traveled alone to London, England. She was going to attend more meetings and was happy to be in a country where people spoke English. When she arrived in London, she tried to arrange an interview with the German emperor, Wilhelm II. He was visiting London to talk about disarmament, or decreasing the number of weapons of war. His assistants ignored Lockwood's request. She was more successful in her efforts to speak with British leaders. Some of them took Lockwood to visit the Inns of Court, the place where British lawyers trained, and where they gathered to talk and dine with one another. Later that day, Lockwood wrote home with great excitement to say she had seen Queen Victoria entering her carriage.

Lockwood was quite a celebrity in England, where women were also fighting to win the right to vote. Many knew about her struggle to become a lawyer and her fight with the justices of the Supreme Court. They were also impressed with her brave run for the presidency. Lockwood gave a long interview to a woman reporter. The reporter later wrote that this American patriot was very bright and full of humor and that her face, when speaking, "lights up." Lockwood offered her much-repeated advice, "Teach girls to be self-supporting and you conquer everything."

Lockwood was bursting with stories to tell her friends and family when she arrived back in the United States. Back at work in her law office, she wrote lectures about the people she had met in Paris and London and the things they had talked about. She told everyone that she loved traveling and that she never got seasick.

That was a good thing because the next summer, when Lockwood returned to Europe, her ship ran into a huge storm. Most of the passengers lay on their beds and prayed for the crashing seas to die down, but Lockwood felt fine. She seemed to have been born with sea legs.

Lockwood enjoyed her work with European peace groups. But she knew that until women won the right to vote in the United States, she was needed at home. In the 1890s, when she was not working on legal matters, Lockwood divided her time between the fight for peace and the fight for woman suffrage. When she lectured about peace, she predicted that war was a thing of the past. She talked about how governments could use international courts to prevent wars. She noted that there should be statues and monuments honoring peacemakers, not just generals and admirals. She argued that having schoolboys practice military drill was wrong because it encouraged a love of war. She felt that women had a particular understanding of how to free the world from war. In 1899 she urged President William McKinley to send a woman delegate to an important peace conference being held in the Dutch city of The Hague. The president dismissed her idea and sent five men.

The men who became president of the United States right before and after 1900—Grover Cleveland, William McKinley, Theodore Roosevelt, and William Howard Taft—were stubbornly opposed to a woman's right to vote. Lockwood and her associates tried many different ways to convince them that this was wrong and against the spirit of democracy. Some women campaigned to win the right to vote through a change in their state laws. Other women argued before Congress that women should at least be permitted to vote for president and members of Congress. Still others lobbied for a change in the U.S. Constitution. It was discouraging when nothing seemed to work. On January 1, 1900, people all over the United States celebrated the arrival of the twentieth century. But all the firecrackers, parties, and thoughts about the United States being a modern country did not bring women the right to vote.

Lockwood's mental strength was tested in other ways in the years before 1900. Shortly after she returned from Europe, her little mischief-loving

City Hall in New York City was lit up to celebrate the coming of the twentieth century.

granddaughter Inez died. Lockwood had loved having Inez in her office and missed her very much. She felt blessed when Lura had another child, a boy named DeForest, after his father. Young DeForest played with toy wagons on the floor and made his grandmother laugh. Even though Lockwood was in her sixties, everybody said she was a lively woman. Having a little boy around was perfect for someone with her energy.

One day in 1894 Lura complained of not feeling well. Before anyone could send for help, she collapsed in her bedroom and died with family members standing nearby. Lockwood was a strong woman, but losing the daughter she loved and worked with was very difficult for her. After Lura's death, her husband and little DeForest stayed on at the house on F Street. Three-year-old DeForest was good medicine for everyone in a home that, for a while, was a sad place.

CHAPTER EIGHT

ALWAYS A FIGHTER

Lockwood was a woman who always said and did what she thought was right. She was not rude, but being truthful was important to her, even if her words did not win her friends. Her decision to run for the presidency had delighted many women. Some even named their children after her. But other women had been upset with her political campaigning. They said she entered the political race only to get attention. In fact, Lockwood ran because she strongly believed that women had to show that they were willing to get involved in politics.

Susan B. Anthony had let it be known that she no longer approved of Lockwood after she ran for president. At the end of the nineteenth century, Anthony used her power to prevent Lockwood from having a greater influence in the women's rights movement. In spite of this, Lockwood, always a fighter, continued to lobby for women's right to vote. She worked with a circle of friends who liked her ideas and ways of doing things. Lockwood and her friends argued to members of Congress that no new state should be admitted to the Union that did not permit women to vote. They also argued that women at least should be able to vote for members of the U.S. House of Representatives. (Senators were not yet elected directly by voters.)

Sometimes the women talked to the congressmen in their offices. Several times, however, Lockwood had the opportunity to make a formal argument in front of a congressional committee. She welcomed these opportunities because newspaper reporters usually covered these public meetings. The newpaper articles let readers know that suffrage crusaders would not quit until they had won the right to vote.

In October 1900, Lockwood celebrated her seventieth birthday. She loved birthdays and often invited friends to her house to share a special cake. Little DeForest also loved a good birthday celebration. That year the party was small and quiet. Lockwood's mother, Hannah Bennett, had died in July, and little DeForest's father was ill. Soon after Lockwood's birthday, he, too, died. Lura's son, not quite ten years old, was an orphan. He remained with Lockwood, his Nannie, and continued to go to school in Washington.

Most people hope to stop working by the time they are seventy years old. Lockwood was a sensible woman who had saved and invested for her old age. Still, she had outlived Lura and her husband, and now had DeForest to look after. It was a good thing that she loved being a lawyer, because she could not afford to retire.

The legal business she handled generally involved men and women who also lived in Washington, D.C. But after her seventieth birthday, Lockwood became the lawyer for the Eastern Cherokee Indian Nation. This case became the most important one of her long career.

The people of the Cherokee Nation had long lived in the southeastern part of North America, on land in present-day North Carolina, Tennessee, and Georgia. They hunted, sold deerskins, farmed, and later, when English settlers came to the area, started trading stations. They lived well. In a way, this became their curse. English and then American settlers grew envious of their fertile land. The Cherokee gave quite a bit of territory to their white neighbors. But this goodwill did not satisfy the neighbors. They asked the government in Washington to move all of the Cherokee west of the Mississippi River and to grant them the Cherokee's land. After angry debates in 1838, the U.S. government ordered its soldiers to forcibly remove the Cherokee to the Oklahoma Territory. U.S. soldiers pointed their bayonets at Cherokee men, women, and children. They had no choice but to make the long walk to the West or die. The Cherokee called this forced march *Nunna dual Isunyi*, or the "Trail Where We Cried" (sometimes called the Trail of Tears).

The U.S. government took Cherokee land but promised in treaties to pay small amounts for it and for the houses, barns, and animals that the Cherokee left behind. Not every Cherokee received their money, however. One group of Cherokee had hidden in the mountains and not crossed to Oklahoma. This group hired Lockwood. Although sixty years had passed, they still had not been given the money they considered rightfully theirs.

Lockwood was excited at the thought of helping the Cherokee, some of whom had come to live in Washington and become her friends. She discussed the history of the Cherokee people and treaty rights with them.

After Congress passed the Indian Removal Act in 1830, President Andrew Jackson stated that "emigration should be voluntary." Nevertheless, thousands of Cherokee made the hard journey westward against their will in 1838 and 1839.

Lockwood went to work on this case as soon as she was hired. From 1901 to 1906, she wrote many long legal arguments, called briefs. In them she explained how the rights of her clients had been violated and why they were owed as much as several million dollars. Several times she had to make these arguments in court, always speaking before panels of male judges. The big day for Lockwood and her Cherokee clients came on January 16, 1906. On that day, the justices of the U.S. Supreme Court heard her case. Lockwood made a long oral argument. Later, she wrote a Cherokee friend, "My speech before the Supreme Court has been highly complimented by the Judges."

Indeed, she had made a good argument. Her Cherokee clients won their case. They shared in a

five-million-dollar settlement from the U.S. government. Lockwood was jubilant, happy for the
Cherokee and for herself. She had been clever in
figuring out how to win and knew that the victory
would help her reputation and that of all women lawyers. In 1906, despite Lockwood's trail blazing, there
were fewer than three hundred female lawyers in the
United States. And only two dozen of them were
permitted to argue cases before the Supreme Court.
By comparison, there were nearly one hundred thousand male attorneys in the United States at the time
Lockwood won the Cherokee case.

Lockwood celebrated the hard-won victory by taking DeForest on a trip to Europe. He was fifteen and
quite a bit taller than his grandmother. They first went
to Milan, Italy, where Lockwood attended an international peace meeting. She was happy to join with the
other delegates in applauding Bertha von Suttner of
Austria. Suttner had just received the Nobel Peace
Prize, the first woman to have that honor. She had
organized peace groups in Austria and written books
critical of warlike nations.

When the meeting ended, Lockwood and DeForest
boarded a train and went sightseeing in Italy. They
traveled south to Rome. DeForest looked forward
to seeing the Colosseum. In ancient Roman times,
bloody gladiator contests were held in this amphi-
theater before as many as fifty thousand spectators.
Lockwood and DeForest walked all over the city
visiting monuments, gardens, and the Sistine Chapel.
Four hundred years earlier, artist Michelangelo had

Bertha von Suttner *(right)* was a leading figure in the peace movement. She published the novel *Die Waffen nieder!* (*Lay Down Your Arms!*) in 1889 and founded an Austrian pacifist organization in 1891. She was awarded the Nobel Peace Prize in 1905. Lockwood was in Europe to celebrate Suttner's many accomplishments.

climbed ladders and scaffolds sixty feet above the ground in order to paint stories from the Bible's Book of Genesis on the chapel ceiling.

On the boat sailing home, Lockwood may have thought that she would never again visit Europe. She was, after all, weeks from celebrating her seventy-sixth birthday. Her life had been exciting and busy and perhaps she imagined that there would be less to do and that she would travel less frequently. But, in fact, the next ten years of her life were incredibly busy.

Lockwood took many trips to Oklahoma and North Carolina to see that her Cherokee clients received their share of the five-million-dollar settlement. In 1909 Syracuse University in upstate New York honored

Lockwood at its graduation ceremony, making her a doctor of law. At the ceremony, she was given a large white silk diploma on which was printed, "Belva Ann Lockwood Legum Doctorem Universitas Syracusana, MCMIX." Lockwood was one of the first American women to receive such an honor. Afterward, she spoke of it with pride.

Lockwood also held yearly birthday parties. She always joked about her age. In 1910 Lockwood told

Lockwood was proud of the honorary doctor of law degree that she received in 1909 from Syracuse University in New York. Afterward, she often posed with this diploma and in her official cap and gown. Here she is shown with other members of the American Woman's Republic (AWR), Mabel G. Lewis *(left)* and the Reverend Susanna Harris *(right)*.

a visiting reporter, "I've never had an eightieth birth-day before, and I'll never have another one, so I just said to myself 'You deserve a day off, and a birthday cake, too!'"

In 1913, when she was eighty-three, Lockwood returned to Europe. She led a group of women who had been studying politics and who were concerned about the possibility of war breaking out in Europe. One of the stops on their tour was Budapest, Hungary. During their stay there, Lockwood accepted an invitation to record a message of peace on the newly invented radiotelegraph machine.

Although she was in her eighties, she was still practicing law. In one case, she went to court and cleared Mary E. Gage, a wealthy Washington

Lockwood *(front row, second from left)* poses with other members of the AWR, a civic organization, during their trip to the International Woman Suffrage Alliance Congress in Budapest, Hungary, in 1913. This was Lockwood's last trip overseas.

woman, of charges that she had threatened to kill a well-known local banker. Lockwood's friends thought so highly of her work that they raised the money to pay Boston artist Nellie Mathes Horne to paint her portrait, which was given to the National Portrait Gallery in Washington.

In 1914, at another of Lockwood's birthday celebrations, a reporter asked her whether a woman would one day be president. She had certainly thought a great deal about that question. She reminded him that the people of the United States had still not approved a change to the U.S. Constitution giving women the right to vote. She was an optimist, however, and thought that there would soon be a woman suffrage amendment. She also believed that women would be elected to Congress before being elected president. Lockwood told him that it was not enough that some women wanted to see a woman in the White House. For a woman to hold that high office, she said, she must prove herself "mentally fit for the position." She did not need to tell him that back in 1884, Belva Lockwood had been more than ready to be the first woman president of the United States.

Belva Lockwood continued to march for suffrage and international peace until her final illness. She died in Washington, D.C., on May 19, 1917. She was eighty-six years old.

The National Portrait Gallery in Washington, D.C., displays this portrait of Belva Lockwood wearing academic robes. Artist Nellie Mathes Horne painted it in 1913.

WHO COULD VOTE AND WHO COULD NOT?

All her life, Belva Lockwood fought hard to win women the right to vote. It was not an easy fight. Even at the beginning of the twentieth century, people were still not certain that women should get involved in the "dirty business" of politics. Men and some women were still nervous about how women would use their votes: Would they outlaw war or use money to build schools instead of roads? Would they forbid the sale of alcohol?

The biggest problem lay in the fact that the U.S. Constitution was silent on the question of whether women could vote. Nothing in its words said women could vote. No words said they could not. Most people thought that the Constitution left it up to the state governments to determine who might vote in elections for Congress and the presidency, as well as in local contests. And so, in the nineteenth century, as women began to demand the right to vote, many reformers assumed that permission would have to be given by the states, even if voting in a federal election was involved. These people decided that they would have to wage state-by-state campaigns to win woman suffrage.

Other women, including Susan B. Anthony, Elizabeth Cady Stanton, and Belva Lockwood, thought that convincing each state to pass a woman suffrage law would take forever. They urged an amendment to the U.S. Constitution itself. They wanted this amendment to say that neither the United States (national) government nor the state governments could deny women the right to vote.

In the late nineteenth century and the first years of the twentieth century, women fought for suffrage using both strategies. Some reformers worked to get the states to change their suffrage laws. Other activists lobbied the U.S. Congress to start the process needed to amend the national constitution. Some states—and even towns and counties—did pass laws that permitted women to vote. Sometimes a new law only permitted women to vote in a school board election, for mayor, or for governor. But other states let women living within their borders vote in federal and state elections. So for a while, women could vote in some parts of the United States, while in other places they could not. These differences were sometimes confusing and, many women believed, unfair. They did not think that where you lived should determine whether you could vote.

Finally, in 1920, the Nineteenth Amendment to the U.S. Constitution became law. It was the change that Belva Lockwood and her friends had wanted: that "the right of citizens of the United States to vote shall not be denied or abridged by the United States or any state on account of sex."

In 1920, three years after Lockwood's death, American women finally won the right to vote. Suffragist Alice Paul *(above in balcony)* and other members of the National Woman's Party celebrate the passage of the Nineteenth Amendment to the Constitution guaranteeing women the right to vote.

Lockwood died before this change to the Constitution was ratified. Despite her many accomplishments, she was never permitted to vote. And when she died, in 1917, it was still very difficult for women to win admission to law school. Slowly this has changed. In the twenty-first century, women make up half of most law school classes. More women are being chosen as judges.

Although Belva Lockwood first argued a case before the U.S. Supreme Court in 1880, the first woman Supreme Court justice, Sandra Day O'Connor, was not appointed until 1981. Twelve years later, in 1993, Ruth Bader Ginsburg joined her as the second woman on the Court. When O'Connor retired in 2006, Justice Ginsburg remained as the only woman out of nine justices serving on the Supreme Court.

TIMELINE

1830 Belva is born on October 24.

1844 Belva is hired as a local schoolteacher.

1848 Belva marries Uriah McNall.

1849 Daughter Lura is born.

1853 Uriah dies. Belva studies at Gasport Academy.

1854 Belva enters Genesee College.

1857 Belva graduates with honors. She begins teaching in Lockport, New York.

1863 Belva runs Owego Female Institute in Owego, New York.

1866 Belva moves to Washington, D.C. She opens McNall's Seminary.

1868 Belva marries the Reverend Ezekiel Lockwood.

1869 Jessie Belva Lockwood is born. Belva's application to law school is rejected.

1870 The National Woman Suffrage Association holds its first convention in Washington, D.C. Belva works for passage of the Arnell Bill. Jessie dies.

1871 Belva enrolls in National University Law School.

1872 Belva twice passes tests but is denied graduation. She travels South as a journalist.

1873 Belva is admitted to the District of Columbia bar association.

1877 Belva buys a house in downtown Washington. Ezekiel dies.

1879 On March 3, Belva is sworn in as the first woman attorney to become a member of the U.S. Supreme Court bar.

1880 Belva proposes African American attorney Samuel R. Lowery for membership in the U.S. Supreme Court bar.
She is the first woman lawyer to argue a case at the Supreme Court.

1884 Belva runs for president for the Equal Rights Party. She starts touring as a lecturer.

1888 Belva runs again for president.

1889 Belva travels to Paris for the Universal Peace Union.

1894 Lura dies.

1900 Belva begins to represent Cherokees in U.S. court.

1906 Belva wins case for Cherokees.

1913 Belva records a peace message in Budapest, Hungary.

1917 Belva Lockwood dies May 19.

BELVA LOCKWOOD'S ACCEPTANCE LETTER

Thirty-six years before the Nineteenth Amendment to the U. S. Constitution guaranteed women the right to vote, Belva Lockwood ran for the presidency. She made the decision to be a candidate precisely because women were not permitted to vote. In her words, she wanted to "make Americans conscious of women's right to political equality." Like any male candidate, Lockwood accepted the nomination of her party with a statement of campaign ideas. Her letter, reproduced below, was originally handwritten, thirteen pages in length. The original is in the Princeton University Library in Princeton, New Jersey, and the letter is reprinted with their permission:

619 F St., N. W.
Wash. D.C. Sept. 3, 1884

Marietta L. Stow Pres.
Eliza C. Webb Sec
and members of the National
Equal Rights Party!

Mesdames,

Having been duly notified of your action in Convention assembled of Aug. 23rd 1884 in nominating me as the candidate for the high position of Chief Magistrate [President] of the United States as the choice of the Equal Rights Party; although feeling unworthy and incompetent to fill so high a place, I am constrained to accept the nomination so generously and enthusiastically tendered by the only political party who really and trully [sic] represent the interests of our whole people North, South, East and West, because I believe that with your unanimous and cordial support, and the fairness and justice of our cause; we shall not only be able to carry the election, but to guide the Ship of State safely into port.

In the furtherance of this purpose I have to say that should it be my good fortune to be elected, and should our party with its grand platform of principles be successful in the contemplated election, it will be my earnest effort to promote and maintain equal political privileges to every class of our citizens irrespective of sex, color or nationality, and to make of this great and glorious Country in truth what it has so long been in name, "the land of the free and the home of the brave."

I shall seek to insure a fair distribution of the public offices to women as well as to men, with a scrupulous regard to civil service reform after the women are duly installed in office.

I am also in accord with the platform of the party in the desire to protect and foster American industries, and in my sympathy with the working men and women of the country, who are organized against free trade, for the purpose of rendering the laboring classes of our country comfortable and independent.

I sympathize with the soldier and the soldier's widow;— . . . believing that the surplus revenues of the country cannot be better used than in clothing the widows and educating the orphans of our Nation's defenders. I would also suggest the abolishment of the Pension Office with its complicated and technical machinery, which so beautifully illustrates how not to do it, and recommend in its stead three Commissioners, whose only duty should consist in requiring from an applicant for invalid pension his Certificate of honorable discharge, from a widow proof of marriage, and from a mother proof of birth.

I am opposed to monopoly in the sense of the men of the country monopolizing all of the votes and all of the offices, and at the same time insisting upon having the distribution of all of the money both public and private. It is this sort of monopoly that has made possible large breaches of trust with government officials. . . . It has engendered and fostered strikes.

I am opposed to the wholesale monopoly of the judiciary of the country by the male voters. If elected, I shall feel it incumbent on me to appoint a reasonable number of women as District Attorneys, Marshals and Judges of United States Courts, and would appoint some competent woman to any vacancy that might occur on the United States Supreme Bench.

I am in full sympathy with the Temperance advocates of the country, especially the N. C. T. U. [a temperance organization], but believe that Woman Suffrage will have a greater tendency to abolish the liquor traffic, than prohibition will to bring about woman suffrage. If the former is adopted, the latter will be its probable sequence.

If elected, I shall recommend in my Inaugural speech, a uniform system of laws as far as practicable for all of the States, and especially for marriage, divorce, and the limitation of contracts, and such a regulation of the laws of descent and distribution of estates as will make the wife equal with the husband in authority and right, and an equal partner in the common business.

I favor an extension of our commercial relations with foreign countries, and especially with the Central and South American States, and the establishment of a high Court of Arbitration to which shall be referred all differences that may arise between these several States, or between them and the United States.

My Indian policy would be, to break up their tribal relations, distribute to them their lands. . . , and make them citizens, amenable to the laws of the land as other white and colored persons are. . . .

Again thanking you Ladies for your expressions of esteem, I think that I may safely say that I fully endorse your whole platform.

Cordially yours,
Belva A. Lockwood

SOURCE NOTES

9 Belva Ann Lockwood, "My Efforts to Become a Lawyer," *Lippincott's Magazine,* February 1888, 215.

15 Ibid., 216.

15 Ibid.

17 Belva Ann Lockwood, "Belva A. Lockwood," Autobiographical Manuscript Sent to Susan B. Anthony for *Johnson's New Universal Cyclopaedia,* July 24, 1876. Papers of E. C. Stanton and S. B. Anthony, 18:938–941, Library of Congress.

18 Lockwood, "My Efforts," 216.

18 Belva A. Lockwood, "The Women Who Tried to Vote," *Lockport (NY) Daily Journal,* May 13, 1871, 1.

19 Lockwood, "My Efforts," 216–217.

20 Lockwood, "Belva A. Lockwood."

21 Lockwood, "My Efforts," 217.

21 Lockwood, "Belva A. Lockwood."

28 Lockwood, "My Efforts," 218.

30 Kathleen Barry, *Susan B. Anthony: A Biography of a Singular Feminist* (New York: New York University Press, 1988), 113.

32 Lockwood, "My Efforts," 220.

36 Alan Lessoff, *The Nation and Its City* (Baltimore: Johns Hopkins University Press, 1994), 17.

36 Lockwood, "My Efforts," 221.

38 Ibid.

41 Ibid., 222.

42 Ibid.

44 Allen C. Clarke, "Belva Ann Lockwood," *Records of the Columbia Historical Society 35–36,* 1935, 207.

44 Lockwood, "My Efforts," 222.

44 Lockwood, "The Women Who Tried to Vote," 1.

45 Lockwood, "My Efforts," 222.

49–50 Lockwood, "The Women Who Tried to Vote," 1.

51 Lockwood, "My Efforts," 222–223.

51 Ibid., 223.

53 Ibid.

55 Belva Lockwood, "Humphreys' Adminx. v. the U.S Chief,"

6, Lockwood papers, Swarthmore College Peace Collection, Swarthmore, PA.

55–56 Lockwood, "My Efforts," 224.

60 *Washington Post,* "Belva Mounts Her Pegasus," March 7, 1882, Belva Lockwood File, Historical Society of Washington, DC.

61 Malvina Shanklin Harlin, *Some Memories of a Long Life, 1854–1911* (New York: Modern Library, 2002), 100.

62 Ibid.

62–63 *New York World,* "Belva Lockwood, 82 Years Young," November 3, 1912, N5.

65 Lura McNall, "Our Washington Letter," *Lockport (NY) Daily Journal,* February 11, 1880, 2.

71 *Washington Evening Star,* "For Belva and Reform," September 17, 1884, 1.

73 *Cincinnati Commercial Gazette,* "Belva Lockwood's High Self-Esteem," October 19, 1884, 6.

76 *Washington Evening Star,* "Poem," September 26, 1884, 4.

76 *Frank Leslie's Illustrated Newspaper,* "Woman in Politics," September 20, 1884, 72, 74–75.

79 Lecture advertisement, "Belva Lockwood, the Eminent Barrister of Washington, D.C.," the Lockwood/Ormes Collection, National Museum of American History, Smithsonian Institution, Washington, DC.

80 *New York World,* "Woman's Part in Politics: Mrs. Belva A. Lockwood Talks about Herself to Nellie Bly," August 12, 1888, 13:3.

80 Brooke Kroeger, *Nellie Bly: Daredevil, Reporter, Feminist* (New York: Times Books, 1994).

83 "Opinions of the Press," January 29, 1892, 2, in the Lockwood/Ormes Collection, National Museum of American History, Smithsonian Institution, Washington, D.C.

84 Helena B. Temple, "Interview," *Women's Penny Paper,* October 5, 1889, 1.

91–92 Belva Lockwood to John M. Taylor, letter, May 7, 1906, Taylor Papers, Duke University, Durham, NC.

95 "Eighty Years Old Is Mrs. Lockwood," 1910 newspaper clipping, Lockwood Papers, Swarthmore College Peace Collection.

96 Harold B. Johnson, interview, *Watertown (NY) Daily Times,* November 7, 1914, 40.

SELECTED BIBLIOGRAPHY

Babcock, Barbara Allen. "Clara Shortridge Foltz: 'First Woman.'" *Arizona Law Review,* 1988, 673–717.

Drachman, Virginia G. *Sisters in Law: Women Lawyers in Modern American History.* Cambridge, MA: Harvard University Press, 1998.

———. *Women Lawyers and the Origins of Professional Identity in America: The Letters of the Equity Club, 1887 to 1890.* Ann Arbor: University of Michigan Press, 1993.

Friedman, Jane M. *America's First Woman Lawyer: The Biography of Myra Bradwell.* Buffalo: Prometheus Books, 1993.

Gabriel, Mary. *Notorious Victoria: The Life of Victoria Woodhull, Uncensored.* Chapel Hill, NC: Algonquin Books, 1998.

Goldsmith, Barbara. *Other Powers.* New York: Knopf, 1998.

Gordon, Ann D., ed. *The Selected Papers of Elizabeth Cady Stanton and Susan B. Anthony.* Vols. 1–4. New Brunswick, NJ: Rutgers University Press, 1997–2006.

Keyssar, Alexander. *The Right to Vote: The Contested History of Democracy in the United States.* New York: Basic Books, 2000.

Lockwood, Belva A. "A Female President: Shall We Ever Have One in the United States?" *The Illustrated American,* May 24, 1890.

———. "How I Ran for the Presidency." *National Magazine,* March 1903, 728–733.

———. "My Efforts to Become a Lawyer." *Lippincott's Magazine,* February 1888, 215–229.

Mossman, Mary Jane. *First Women Lawyers: A Comparative Study of Gender, Law, and the Legal Profession.* Portland, OR: Hart Publisher, 2006.

Norgren, Jill. *Belva Lockwood: The Woman Who Would Be President.* New York: New York University Press, 2007.

Stanton, Elizabeth Cady, Susan B. Anthony, and Matilda Joslyn Gage, eds. *History of Woman Suffrage.* 1881–1922. Reprint, New York: Arno Press, 1969.

Stern, Madeleine B. "Belva Lockwood." In *We the Women.* 1963. Reprint, Lincoln: University of Nebraska Press, 1994.

Underhill, Lois Beachy. *The Woman Who Ran for President.* Bridgehampton, NY: Bridge Works, 1995.

Winner, Julia Hull. *Belva A. Lockwood.* Lockport, NY: Niagara County Historical Society, 1969.

FURTHER READING AND WEBSITES

Books

Guernsey, JoAnn Bren. *Hillary Rodham Clinton.* Minneapolis: Twenty-First Century Books, 2005.

Havelin, Kate. *Victoria Woodhull: Fearless Feminist.* Minneapolis: Twenty-First Century Books, 2007.

Kendall, Martha E. *Failure Is Impossible!: The History of American Women's Rights.* Minneapolis: Twenty-First Century Books, 2001.

Stuart, Nancy Rubin. *The Muse of the Revolution: The Secret Pen of Mercy Otis Warren and the Founding of a Nation.* Boston: Beacon Press, 2008.

Thimmesh, Catherine. *Madam President.* Boston: Houghton Mifflin Co., 2004.

Websites

Women and Law
http://www.womenslegalhistory.stanford.edu/
The Women's Legal History website that includes biographical information of women lawyers in the United States.

Women and Politics
http://www.cawp.rutgers.edu/Facts.html
The Center for American Women and Politics at Rutgers University website includes information on women candidates and officeholders at national, state, and local levels.

Women and Social Movements
http://womhist.alexanderstreet.com
This website permits readers to view thousands of documents accompanied by explanatory essays about the women and social movements in the United States, 1600–2000.

INDEX

ABOUT THE AUTHOR

Jill Norgren has taught for many years at the City University of New York. She has written several books and textbooks about law, American Indians, and the history of women. Most recently, she wrote a biography of Belva Lockwood for adults. She also writes frequently for political and academic journals and has received awards from the American Society for Legal History and the United States Supreme Court Historical Society. She and her husband have two daughters and three granddaughters. They live in New York City.

PHOTO ACKNOWLEDGMENTS

The images in this book are used with the permission of: Schwimmer-Lloyd Collection/ Manuscripts and Archives Division, New York Public Library, Astor, Lenox and Tilden Foundations, p. 2; © North Wind Picture Archives, pp. 9; 16; Library of Congress, pp. 12 (LC-USZ62-3588), 37 (cai2a14728), 50, 54 (LC-USZC2-2598), 65, 66, 81 (LC-USZC2-758), 86 (LC-USZ62-78693), 100; The Granger Collection, New York, pp. 14, 24, 46, 75; Emmet Collection, Miriam and Ira D. Wallach Division of Art, Prints and Photographs, The New York Public Library, Astor, Lenox and Tilden Foundations, p. 19; © Independent Picture Service, p. 25; © Bettmann/CORBIS, p. 27; Robert N. Dennis collection of stereoscopic views, Miriam and Ira D. Wallach Division of Art, Prints and Photographs, New York Public Library, Astor, Lenox and Tilden Foundations, p. 28; © Hulton Archive/Getty Images, p. 31; Swarthmore College Peace Collection, pp. 34, 82; National Archives (War & Conflict), p. 39; Courtesy of Mrs. Norma Z. Wollenberg, Town of Royalton Historical Society, p. 40; Mary Evans Picture Library, p. 41; Collection of Jill Norgren, p. 60; Ohio Historical Society, p. 62; New York State Historical Association, Cooperstown, p. 64; The Art Archive/Culver Pictures, p. 68; Print Collection, Miriam and Ira D. Wallach Division of Art, Prints and Photographs, The New York Public Library, Astor, Lenox and Tilden Foundations, p. 69; © David J. & Janice L. Frent Collection/CORBIS, p. 70; Collection of Captain John W. Koster, USCG, p. 73; Division of Political History/ Smithsonian Institution, [76-2569], p. 74; National Museum of American History, Smithsonian Institution, p. 79; Woolaroc Museum, Bartlesville, OK, p. 91; AP Photo, p. 93; © Niagara County Historical Society, Lockport, NY , p. 94; Schwimmer-Lloyd collection, Manuscripts and Archives Division, The New York Public Library, Astor, Lenox and Tilden Foundations, p. 95; National Portrait Gallery, Smithsonian Institution/ Swarthmore College Peace Collection, p. 97.

Front Cover: © CORBIS (main); © PhotoDisc/Getty Images (background).